ASCENT®

CENTER FOR TECHNICAL KNOWLEDGE

Autodesk® Inventor® 2018
Surface and Freeform Modeling

Student Guide

Mixed Units - 1st Edition

AUTODESK.
Authorized Publisher

ASCENT - Center for Technical Knowledge®
Autodesk® Inventor® 2018
Surface and Freeform Modeling
Mixed Units - 1st Edition

Prepared and produced by:

ASCENT Center for Technical Knowledge
630 Peter Jefferson Parkway, Suite 175
Charlottesville, VA 22911

866-527-2368
www.ASCENTed.com

Lead Contributor: Jennifer MacMillan

ASCENT - Center for Technical Knowledge is a division of Rand Worldwide, Inc., providing custom developed knowledge products and services for leading engineering software applications. ASCENT is focused on specializing in the creation of education programs that incorporate the best of classroom learning and technology-based training offerings.

We welcome any comments you may have regarding this student guide, or any of our products. To contact us please email: feedback@ASCENTed.com.

AS-INV1801-SFM1MU-SG   //   IS-INV1801-SFM1MU-SG

Contents

Preface

The *Autodesk® Inventor® 2018: Surface and Freeform Modeling* student guide teaches you how to incorporate surfacing and freeform modeling techniques into your design environment.

You begin with instruction on how to create the splines and 3D sketches commonly used in surface creation. Chapters on surface creation focus on using these sketches or existing geometry to create surfaces for use in your solid models. Freeform modeling is also covered, which enables you to create complex shapes without needing the constraints required in a parametric workflow. To complete the student guide, you will learn how to use the Autodesk Inventor surface analysis tools to evaluate the continuity between surfaces and the curvature on a surface, determine if the applied draft is within a specified range, and conduct section analysis to evaluate wall thickness values.

The topics covered in this student guide are also covered in ASCENT's *Autodesk® Inventor® 2018: Advanced Part Modeling* student guide, which includes a broader range of advanced learning topics.

Objectives

- Create spline and 3D sketched entities.

- Create planar and three-dimensional surfaces.

- Combine individual surface features into a single quilted surface.

- Add or remove material in a model by referencing a surface.

- Create solid geometry using surface geometry.

- Remove portions of a surface using a reference surface or work plane.

- Manipulate the extent of a surface by extending or stretching it.

- Create a new solid face by replacing an existing solid face with surface geometry.

- Remove existing surfaces or solid faces from a model.

- Copy surfaces from one model into another.

- Create freeform geometry base shapes, faces, and converted geometry.

- Edit freeform base geometry by manipulating existing geometry or adding new elements to the base shape.

- Use the surface analysis tools to evaluate continuity between surfaces, check draft values, analyze curvature on a surface, and review sectioned areas of the model.

Note on Software Setup

This student guide assumes a standard installation of the software using the default preferences during installation. Lectures and practices use the standard software templates and default options for the Content Libraries.

Students and Educators can Access Free Autodesk Software and Resources

Autodesk challenges you to get started with free educational licenses for professional software and creativity apps used by millions of architects, engineers, designers, and hobbyists today. Bring Autodesk software into your classroom, studio, or workshop to learn, teach, and explore real-world design challenges the way professionals do.

Get started today - register at the Autodesk Education Community and download one of the many Autodesk software applications available.

Visit www.autodesk.com/joinedu/

Note: Free products are subject to the terms and conditions of the end-user license and services agreement that accompanies the software. The software is for personal use for education purposes and is not intended for classroom or lab use.

Lead Contributor: Jennifer MacMillan

With a dedication for engineering and education, Jennifer has spent over 20 years at ASCENT managing courseware development for various CAD products. Trained in Instructional Design, Jennifer uses her skills to develop instructor-led and web-based training products as well as knowledge profiling tools.

Jennifer has achieved the Autodesk Certified Professional certification for Inventor and is also recognized as an Autodesk Certified Instructor (ACI). She enjoys teaching the training courses that she authors and is also very skilled in providing technical support to end-users.

Jennifer holds a Bachelor of Engineering Degree as well as a Bachelor of Science in Mathematics from Dalhousie University, Nova Scotia, Canada.

Jennifer MacMillan has been the Lead Contributor for *Autodesk Inventor: Surface and Freeform Modeling* since its initial release in 2017.

In this Guide

The following images highlight some of the features that can be found in this Student Guide.

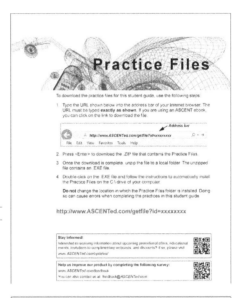

FTP link for practice files

Practice Files

The Practice Files page tells you how to download and install the practice files that are provided with this student guide.

Chapters

Each chapter begins with a brief introduction and a list of the chapter's Learning Objectives.

Learning Objectives for the chapter

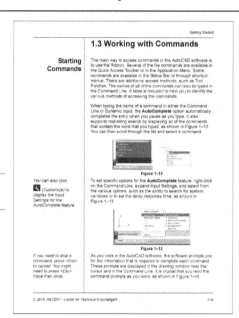

Instructional Content

Each chapter is split into a series of sections of instructional content on specific topics. These lectures include the descriptions, step-by-step procedures, figures, hints, and information you need to achieve the chapter's Learning Objectives.

Side notes

Side notes are hints or additional information for the current topic.

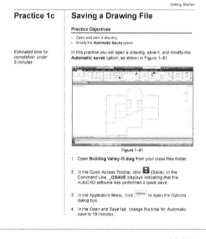

Practice Objectives

Practices

Practices enable you to use the software to perform a hands-on review of a topic.

Some practices require you to use prepared practice files, which can be downloaded from the link found on the Practice Files page.

Chapter Review Questions

Chapter review questions, located at the end of each chapter, enable you to review the key concepts and learning objectives of the chapter.

Command Summary

The Command Summary is located at the end of each chapter. It contains a list of the software commands that are used throughout the chapter, and provides information on where the command is found in the software.

Icons in this Student Guide

The following icons are used to help you quickly and easily find helpful information.

	Indicates items that are new in the Autodesk Inventor 2018 software.
	Indicates items that have been enhanced in the Autodesk Inventor 2018 software.

Practice Files

To download the practice files for this student guide, use the following steps:

1. Type the URL shown below into the address bar of your Internet browser. The URL must be typed **exactly as shown**. If you are using an ASCENT ebook, you can click on the link to download the file.

Address bar

http://www.ascented.com/getfile?id=inolesco

File   Edit   View   Favorites   Tools   Help

2. Press <Enter> to download the .ZIP file that contains the Practice Files.

3. Once the download is complete, unzip the file to a local folder. The unzipped file contains an .EXE file.

4. Double-click on the .EXE file and follow the instructions to automatically install the Practice Files on the C:\ drive of your computer.

   Do not change the location in which the Practice Files folder is installed. Doing so can cause errors when completing the practices in this student guide.

http://www.ascented.com/getfile?id=inolesco

Stay Informed!

Interested in receiving information about upcoming promotional offers, educational events, invitations to complimentary webcasts, and discounts? If so, please visit:

www.ASCENTed.com/updates/

Help us improve our product by completing the following survey:

www.ASCENTed.com/feedback

You can also contact us at: *feedback@ASCENTed.com*

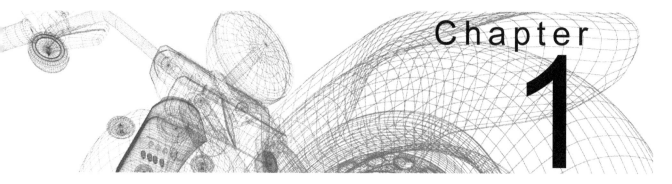

Chapter

1

Sketching Tools

The fundamental level sketch entities that can be created in a 2D sketch include lines, arcs, rectangles, etc. The Spline options provide additional flexibility to create smooth curved entities for creating geometry. Splines and entities such as lines and arcs can also be created in a 3D sketch. 3D sketches enable you to create entities that exist in 3D space without a sketch plane. Along with splines, lines, and arcs, there are a number of additional 3D sketch tools that can be used to create a sketch to generate complex geometry.

Learning Objectives in this Chapter

- Create a spline entity by placing vertices to define its control frame.
- Create a spline entity by placing points that define the exact spline shape.
- Create a 3D sketch that consists of linear, helical, arc, and bend entities.
- Create a 3D sketch by entering an equation that defines the x, y, and z coordinates over a specified range.
- Create 3D curves that are based on intersections of planes or the projection of geometry onto non-planar surfaces.
- Create a 3D curve that is sketched on a curved face.

1.1 Splines

You can draw curves using Arc and Ellipse entities, but those curves can be too rigid. To create a free-form curve consider using a Spline. There are two types of splines that can be sketched: **Control Vertex** and **Interpolation**.

- For a Control Vertex Spline, the points that are placed to create the spline define the vertices of the control frame. The control frame defines the shape of the spline, as shown in Figure 1–1.

Multiple splines can be sketched and constrained to one another using the

(Smooth (G2)) constraint to produce a smooth transition between entities. This constraint can also be used to constrain a spline to other sketched entities.

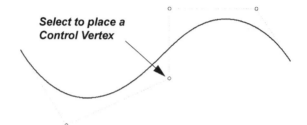

Select to place a Control Vertex

Figure 1–1

- For an Interpolation Spline, the spline is fit through the selected points, as shown in Figure 1–2.

Figure 1–2

You can use splines in models for many purposes, such as a base for creating surfaces, parting lines for splitting molds and drafts, or a sweep path, as shown in Figure 1–3.

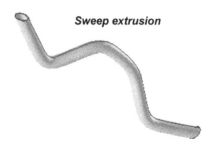

Sweep extrusion

Figure 1–3

How To: Create a Spline

1. Select the type of spline that is required.

The Spline options for a 2D Sketch are located with the line entities on the Create panel.

- In the *Sketch* tab>Create panel, click (Spline Interpolation).
- In the *Sketch* tab>Create panel, click (Spline Control Vertex).
- If creating a spline in 3D sketch, the commands are located in the *3D Sketch* tab>Draw panel, in their own drop-down list.

2. Sketch the free-form spline by placing points or by selecting existing work points, end points, or midpoints.

- An Interpolation spline is sketched by selecting points that will lie on the exact path of the spline.

You cannot add fillets or chamfers to a spline and you cannot select the midpoint of a spline.

- A Control Vertex spline is sketched by selecting points that define the control frame.

Hint: Identifying Spline Points

To help identify splines, the end points of a Interpolation Spline display as a square shape, while the fit points along the curve display as a diamond, as shown in Figure 1–4.

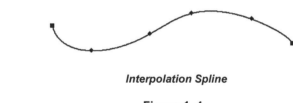

Interpolation Spline

Figure 1–4

---

3. Add dimensions and constraints to the spline's points and control vertices, similar to that shown in Figure 1–5. Interpolation Splines can be dimensioned in a similar way between points.

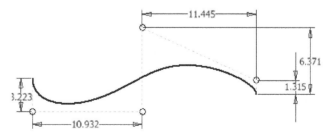

Figure 1–5

---

4. Right-click and select **Create** or click  in the mini-toolbar. You can also select **Cancel [Esc]** to cancel sketching and deactivate the command, or select **Restart** to restart the spline.

Editing a Spline

Once the spline is complete, you can select the spline to edit it as follows:

- Select and drag the shape points (control vertices or interpolation points) to new locations. For Interpolation Splines, if you press and hold <Alt> while dragging, other unconstrained points also move.

- For Interpolation Splines, select and drag the tangent handles displayed at all shape points, as shown in Figure 1–6, to manipulate the shape of the spline. The handle must be activated to modify. To activate a handle, select the shape point, right-click and select **Activate Handle**.

Figure 1–6

You can also edit the spline attributes using options in the shortcut menu. The spline editing options include the following:

- Select **Insert Point** or **Insert Vertex** in the shortcut menu to add additional internal shape points for interpolation or control vertex splines, respectively.

The options available in the shortcut menu depend on whether the spline was created as a control vertex or an interpolation spline. Additionally, where you right-click on the spline can affect which options are displayed.

- Click **Display Curvature** in the marking menu to display a curvature comb that indicates the curvature along the spline, as shown in Figure 1–7. The length of each comb line is inversely proportional to the radius of the curve at that point. If the curvature comb does not display, right-click and select **Setup Curvature Display** to modify the comb's density and scale.

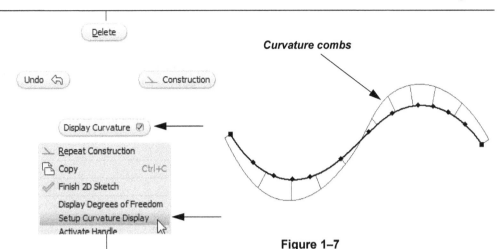

Figure 1–7

The options in the shortcut menu vary depending on whether the spline, point, or handles are selected.

- Select **Activate Handle**, **Curvature**, or **Flat** in the shortcut menu to control the shape of the spline at the shape points. The shape point nearest to where you right-clicked is affected. The spline shown in Figure 1–8 has **Activate Handle** applied to it. This option displays a line tangent to the spline (called a handlebar) on the shape point; adjust the direction of the handlebar by dragging either end. The handlebar rotates about the shape point.

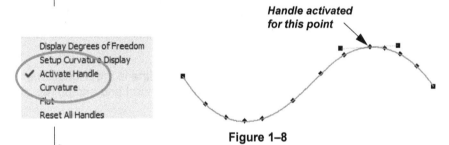

Figure 1–8

- The **Curvature** option provides an arc (called a curvature bar) on the shape point in addition to the tangent line, as shown in Figure 1–9. Drag either end of the curvature bar to change the curvature. The **Flat** option removes the curvature at the selected point.

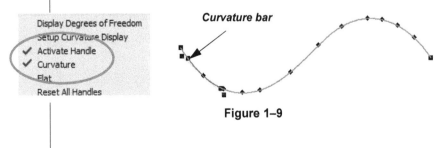

Figure 1–9

- Select **Spline Tension** in the shortcut menu to adjust how straight the spline is between shape points for an interpolation spline. Higher tensions force the spline to become straighter (and the curvature at the shape points becomes tighter). Figure 1–10 shows a spline with zero tension on the left side and maximum (100%) tension on the right side. A start point, end point, and one shape point were used to create the spline.

*If the spline tension is modified, the spline is automatically converted to the **Minimum Energy Fit Method**.*

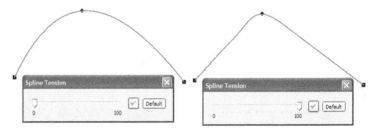

Figure 1–10

- Select **Fit Method** in the shortcut menu to edit the spline transition between shape points in an interpolation spline. The three methods available enable you to create a spline that transitions smoothly between shape points (**Standard**), a spline that uses the AutoCAD fit method (**AutoCAD**), and a spline with smoother continuity and better curvature distribution (**Minimum Energy**). The Minimum Energy method increases the file size and requires longer calculation times.

- Select **Close Spline** in the shortcut menu for an interpolation spline to join the start and end points, as shown in Figure 1–11.

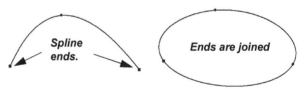

Figure 1–11

- Once spline handles have been reset for an interpolation spline, you can restore all or individual handles to their natural solve state using **Reset All Handles** or **Reset Handle**. The **Reset All Handles** option, as shown in Figure 1–12, is available on the shortcut menu when the spline is selected. The **Reset Handle** option is available on the shortcut menu when a handle is selected.

Resetting a single handle restores it to a natural solve state based on the position of the other handles, not necessarily to its original solve state.

Figure 1–12

- The **Convert to CV Spline** option and **Convert to Interpolation** options enable you to switch a control vertex spline to a spline that was created using interpolation points, and vice versa. The spline shown in Figure 1–13 was originally an interpolation spline that was converted to a Control Vertex spline using **Concert to CV Spline**.

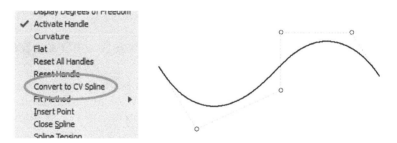

Figure 1–13

1.2 3D Sketches

3D sketches can be used as profiles, rails in a loft, a path to define a 3D sweep, complex surfaces, etc.

While 2D sketching is performed in a plane, 3D sketching takes place in 3D space without a sketch plane. 3D sketches must be drawn from existing points (e.g., work points) or points on existing objects. The 3D sketch is automatically constrained to the selected vertices as it is sketched, as shown in Figure 1–14.

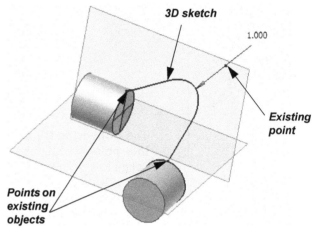

Figure 1–14

How To: Create a 3D sketch

1. In the *3D Model* tab>Sketch panel, click ✎ (Start 3D Sketch). The command can be found on the expanded **Start 2D Sketch** command, as shown in Figure 1–15.

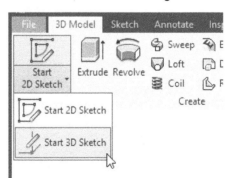

Figure 1–15

2. Use the tools on the *3D Sketch* tab (shown in Figure 1–16) to create 3D entities.

Figure 1–16

3. Modify the entities, as required, using tools on the Modify panel.
4. Using the Constrain panel, add dimensions and constraints to locate the 3D sketched entities, as required.

5. Once you finish sketching, in the Exit panel, click ✔ (Finish Sketch) or select **Finish 3D Sketch** in the context menu.
6. To edit a 3D sketch, right-click on its name in the Model browser and select **Edit 3D Sketch** or double-click on the 3D Sketch in the Model browser.

3D Sketch Tools

The following options in the Draw panel enable you to create entities in a 3D sketch.

Line

To sketch lines, click ✐ (Line) in the Draw panel or right-click and select **Create 3D Line**. Select points to define the line. You can also reference existing work points, sketch points, vertices, and end points. Since 3D sketches are often used to define sweeps for tubing and cabling, the sketch may need to be curved. Auto-Bend places a radius at all corners, as shown in Figure 1–17. To toggle Auto-Bend on or off, right-click and select **Auto-Bend** when creating the Line.

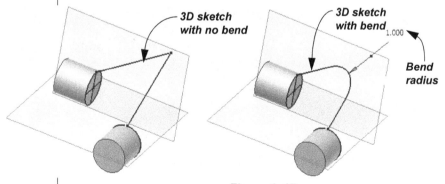

Figure 1–17

- To change the default setting for the Auto-Bend radius for the current file, click ▢ (Document Settings) (*Tools* tab> Options panel), select the *Sketch* tab and change the value in the *Auto-Bend Radius* field. If the radius value is too large for the sketch, the bend is not applied.

> **Hint: Improving Sketch Accuracy**
>
> Consider using the ▢ (Ortho Mode) and ▢ (Snap Object) options in the Status bar at the bottom of the graphics window to better control how the entities are sketched. With **Ortho Mode** enabled, you can restrict sketching to the X, Y, and Z planes. With **Snap Object** enabled, you can snap to existing entities when sketching new entities.

Helical Curve

Click ▢ (Helical Curve) in the Draw panel or right-click and select **Helical Curve** to create a helical or spiral curve. Select a shape type from the menu to define how the curve will be created. The options include the following:

- **Pitch and Revolution**
- **Revolution and Height**
- **Pitch and Height**
- **Spiral**

The options that are available to define the shape depend on the type of curve that was selected. Enter the required values in the Helical Curve dialog box. Once the sizes are entered, select the required point(s) for the curve. You can select these points directly on the model or by entering values in the Inventor Precise Input toolbar. You can also assign the revolution direction by clicking the ▢ and ▢ (Rotation) icons in the dialog box.

Figure 1–18 shows a helical curve and the options used to create it.

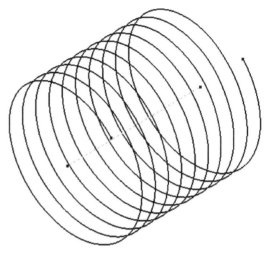

Figure 1–18

Arc

Click ![arc icon] (Arc Three Point) or ![arc icon] + (Arc Center Point) to create an arc as you would in a 2D sketch. The Three Point arc can also be started by right-clicking and then selecting **Three Point Arc**.

Spline

Click ![spline icon] (Spline Interpolation) or ![spline icon] (Spline Control Vertex) to create a spline as you would in a 2D sketch.

> **Hint: Entering Precise Values**
>
> Consider using **Precise Input** in the expanded Draw panel to precisely define the X, Y, and Z location of the entities that are placed in the 3D sketch. This can be used for lines, helical curves, arcs, splines, and points. The Precise Input mini-toolbar enables you to enter values. To close the mini-toolbar once active, expand ![icon] and click **Close**. The interface used for Precise Input varies slightly from that used for 2D sketch creation. In 3D, the interface uses a mini-toolbar.

> **Hint: Aligning and Reorienting the Sketch Triad**
>
> As you are sketching you can right-click and access commands that enable you to align and reorient the model to accurately sketch the entities. The shortcut menu options enable you to do the following:
>
> - **Align to Plane:** Aligns the sketch triad to a plane.
>
> - **Orient Z** and **Orient to World:** Reorients the sketching triad to a custom Z direction or to the world coordinate system. To define a custom Z direction, you can select an edge, line, axis, plane, vertex or point.
>
> - **Snap Intersection:** Snaps an entity to the intersection of entities. This is only available when **Ortho Mode** is enabled.

Equation Curve

An Equation curve enables you to create complex entities by entering an equation that defines the entities path in the X, Y, and Z axes. To create an equation curve, in the Draw panel, click

 (Equation Curve). A mini-toolbar opens, as shown in Figure 1–19, providing you with the fields that you can use to define the curve and the range of values to evaluate.

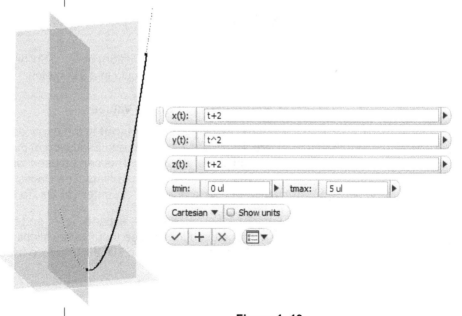

Figure 1–19

Point

Click ╌╎╌ (Point) to create sketch points or center points for use in creating your 3D sketch.

Bend

If you place lines without bends and later decide to add them, click ⌐╎ (Bend) in the Draw panel or right-click and select **Bend**. Enter a radius in the Bend dialog box and select the two lines for the bend to join. The lines to which the bend is applied must meet at a corner.

Intersection Curve

You can create a 3D sketch curve from the intersection of two surfaces, splines, lines, work planes, or parts. The sketch automatically updates if you change either of the two objects.

Click ▨ (Intersection Curve), select the two objects to define the 3D sketch, and click **OK** to create the 3D sketch. If you are using one work plane and another object, select the work plane first. A 3D sketch created by intersecting an extruded surface and the XY Plane is shown in Figure 1–20.

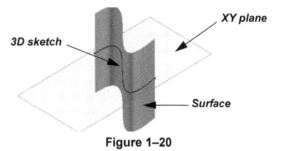

Figure 1–20

Project Curve to Surface

Click (Project to Surface) to create a sketch that is projected onto a face (2D or 3D) from a selected curve(s), as shown in Figure 1–21. The projection output can be along a selected vector, to a closest point, or wrapped to a surface that is flat, cylindrical, or conical.

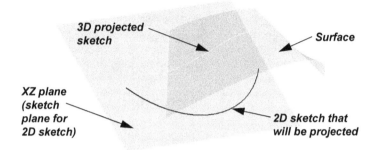

Figure 1–21

Silhouette Curve

A silhouette curve represents the contour of the model relative to a specific pull direction. The curve can include both the inner and outer design model boundaries, as shown in Figure 1–22. The curve can be best explained by imagining a light shining on the model. The curve is placed wherever there is a silhouette.

Silhouette curves are commonly used for generating parting lines for plastic part design, or for use in multi-body part design.

Figure 1–22

Click (Silhouette Curve) and select the *Body* to use as the geometry to create the silhouette curve. In the *Exclusion* area, select whether faces, straight faces, or internal faces are to be excluded from the curve. The curve will be placed on the selected body. Define the *Direction* from which to derive the silhouette curve. The direction can be defined by a plane, face, edge, or axis.

The models shown in Figure 1–23 show two examples of silhouette curves created on similar models. In the left model, the silhouette curve feature creates two curves because the straight faces were excluded, and in the right model, it creates a single curve around the entire model because nothing was excluded.

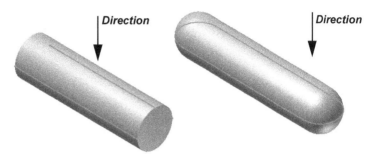

Figure 1–23

Curve on Face

A curve can be sketched directly on a face using the **Curve on Face** command. This enables you to easily locate the sketch directly on a non-planar face without having to project entities. To sketch a curve on a face, click (Curve on Face) in the Draw panel. You can select vertices, edges, or miscellaneous points to define the curve. The curve is placed on the face that is highlighted in red and is generated as a 3D interpolation spline, similar to that shown in Figure 1–24. Once sketched, you have access to the shortcut menu to close the sketch or add additional points. You can also use constraints and dimensions to fully define the curve.

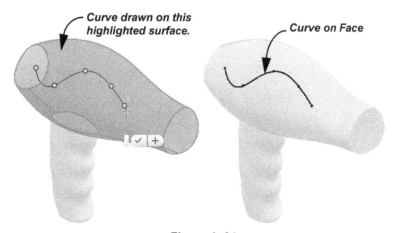

Figure 1–24

Include Geometry

To include edges from 3D objects and 2D sketches in the 3D sketch, click ⬦ (Include Geometry) and select the geometry to include. Alternatively, you can select **Include Geometry** in the shortcut menu to initiate the command. If you change an object that was used with the option, the sketch also updates to reflect this change.

Mirror

Use the ▷|◁ (Mirror) option in the Pattern panel to mirror 3D sketch entities. Like mirroring in a 2D sketch, the mirror plane can be a planar face, an origin plane, or a work plane.

Points

Use the 📑 (Points) option in the Insert panel to insert points from a selected Microsoft Excel file. The requirements for the spreadsheet are:

- Coordinates are on the first sheet.
- Cell A1 lists the unit of measure (a blank cell assumes the default units).
- Row 2 shows column headers (e.g., X, Y, Z).
- Row 3 and thereafter show the coordinates.
- Points reference the sketch origin.

> **Hint: Work Features**
>
> Use the work feature options to create work planes, axis, and points in the 3D Sketch. The Work Feature panel is not displayed by default, you must add it to the panel to use it.

Modifying 3D Sketch Entities

To activate a 3D sketch for editing, double-click on its name in the Model Browser, or select it and

click ⬚ (Edit 3D Sketch).

You can edit using any of the following:

- Select and drag vertices, center points, or any section on a 3D entity to reposition it without entering exact coordinates.

- Double-click on the dimensions to change their value.

- Right-click and select **Construction** to convert a sketched entity into a construction entity.

- Select **Delete** in the shortcut menu to delete an object in the 3D sketch. If you delete an object that was added with the **Include Geometry** option, the source object is not affected.

- Use **Extend**, **Trim**, and **Split** in the Modify panel to refine the sketch's shape. These options are also available when sketching.

- Use **3D Transform** in the Modify panel to reposition geometry in a 3D sketch. Once activated, you are provided with the transform triad and mini-toolbar. Select a manipulator handle on the triad to reposition the selected entity linearly, rotationally, or on a plane. The mini-toolbar updates as required and enables you to enter values to define the move. The mini-toolbar can also be used to control the orientation of the triad to the world, view, or local coordinate systems. In Figure 1–25, a spline entity is being moved along the X axis of the world coordinate system.

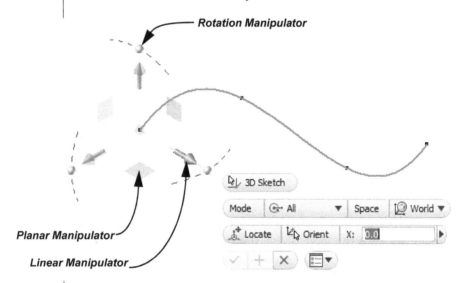

Figure 1–25

Use standard copy and paste functionality to create copies of existing sketched entities in the same sketch or in different sketches. This enables you to efficiently duplicate entities in a 3D sketch. Use the 3D Transform tool to move the pasted entities, as required. If pasted in the same sketch the new entities are pasted over the source entities and must be moved.

Hint: 3D Sketch Properties

The Geometry Properties dialog box, shown in Figure 1–26, can be used in 3D sketches to edit the properties. To open the Geometry Properties dialog box, select the entity, right-click and select **Properties**.

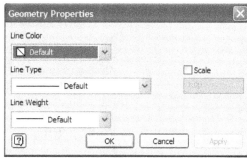

Figure 1–26

Dimensioning & Constraining

Using the Constrain panel, add dimensions and constraints to locate the sketched entities. The dimensions must reference geometry and work points. The available constraint options are shown in Figure 1–27.

Figure 1–27

- The **Coincident**, **Parallel**, **Tangent**, **Collinear**, **Perpendicular**, **Smooth (G2)**, **Fixed**, and **Equal** constraints can be used in the same way as in a 2D sketch.

- The (On Face) constraint enables you to constrain points, lines, arc, or spline to a planar face. Optionally, you can constrain individual points to a curved face.

- The $X_{/\!/}$, $Y_{/\!/}$, and $Z_{/\!/}$ constraint types can be used to constrain a line, curve, or spline handle to lie parallel with the X, Y, or Z axis, respectively.

*Assigned constraints can be deleted by right-clicking on the constraint symbol in the graphics window and selecting **Delete**.*

- The ⬚ , ⬚ , and ⬚ constraint types can be used to constrain a line, curve, or spline to lie parallel with the XY, YZ, or XZ planes, respectively.

When dimensioning and constraining, you can also consider setting the **Dynamic Dimension** and **Infer Constraints** options in the Status Bar to aid in the sketching process.

- ⬚ (Dynamic Dimension): Enables you to toggle whether the dynamic dimension field appears as you are sketching. This field enables you to enter exact values. When disabled, you can only select points to place the entities.

- ⬚ (Infer Constraints): Enables you to control whether constraints are inferred by the Autodesk Inventor software as you are sketching or not.

- ⬚ (Show/Hide Constraints): Enables you to toggle the display of constraint symbols on and off in the sketch.

Practice 1a

Create a Swept Cut using a 3D Sketch

Practice Objectives

- Create a 3D sketch by placing points in the model and using those points to define the location of a 3D spline.
- Create a swept cut that references a sketched profile and a 3D sketched path.

In this practice, you create a swept cut through the model shown on the left of Figure 1–28. You use 3D sketch options to create the path for the sweep. You are provided with work planes and the order in which to create work points that are used to define the 3D sketch. Many of the menu selections are left out so that you can practice feature creation. The final model is shown on the right of Figure 1–28. The model guides a follower while rotating about the X Axis.

 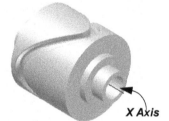

X Axis

Figure 1–28

Task 1 - Create work points.

In this task, you create four work points as the basis for the swept cut's 3D path.

1. In the *Get Started* tab>Launch panel, click (Projects) to open the Projects dialog box. Project files identify folders that contain the required models.

This project file is used for the entire training guide.

2. Click **Browse**. In the *C:\Autodesk Inventor 2018 Design Surface and Freeform Modeling Practice Files* folder, select **Surface and Freeform Modeling.ipj**. Click **Open**. The Projects dialog box updates and a check mark displays next to the new project name, indicating that it is the active project. The project file tells Autodesk Inventor where your files are stored. Click **Done**.

3. Open **barrel_cam.ipt**. The work planes that have been provided will be used as references for the work points that you will create.

4. Create four work points. The planes that will be referenced to create the work points are shown in Figure 1–29.

   - Intersection of the planes 2, 6, and the XY plane.
   - Intersection of the planes 1, 3, and the XZ plane.
   - Intersection of the planes 2, 5, and the XY plane.
   - Intersection of the planes 1, 4, and the XZ plane.

   It is recommended that you select each plane directly in the Model browser to ensure that you are selecting the correct planes. If a work point does not get created after selecting three planes, then one of the planes selected might be incorrect. Most commonly it is due to selecting a plane that does not intersect with the other two.

*Sometimes changing the selection priority to **Feature Priority** and zooming into the model can help to select planes in a model.*

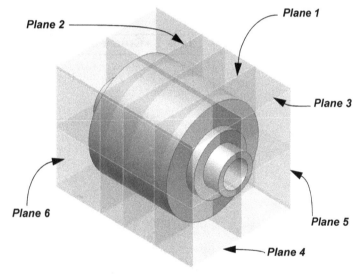

Figure 1–29

5. In the *View* tab>Visibility panel, expand **Object Visibility** and clear the **User Work Planes** and **Origin Planes** options to toggle off the visibility of all work planes and Origin planes.

6. Display the model in Wireframe (*View* tab>Appearance panel>**Visual Style**) and orient the model to the Right view. The model and work points display as shown in Figure 1–30. The model is displayed parallel to the YZ plane.

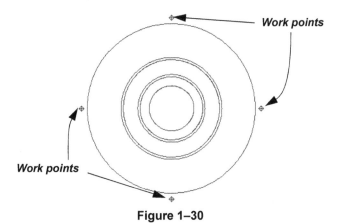

Figure 1–30

Task 2 - Create a 3D sketch.

In this task, you use the 3D sketch options to create the path for the swept cut.

1. Display the model in isometric Home view.

2. Start a 3D sketch by right-clicking and selecting **New 3D Sketch**, or on the ribbon, on the *3D Model* tab, select **Start 3D Sketch**.

3. In the Draw panel, click (Spline Interpolation) and select the existing work points in the order they were created. The model displays as shown in Figure 1–31. You must select the start point a second time to close the spline.

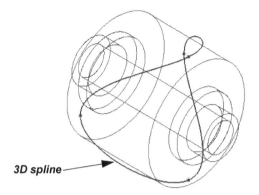

3D spline

Figure 1–31

4. In the Exit panel, click (Finish Sketch).

Task 3 - Create a swept cut profile.

1. Set the three default origin planes as visible.

2. Select the XZ plane in the Model browser, right-click and select **New Sketch** to activate the 2D sketch environment.

3. Project the YZ and XY work planes onto the sketch plane. You use these projected planes to locate and dimension the profile.

4. Project the work point at the intersection of 1, 3, and the XZ plane (Work Point2) onto the sketch plane. The work point location is shown in Figure 1–32. You project the work point because the sweep path must intersect the sketch plane of the profile.

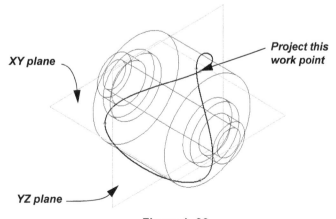

XY plane

Project this work point

YZ plane

Figure 1–32

5. Sketch and dimension the profile, as shown in Figure 1–33. Constrain the sketch to the projected work point.

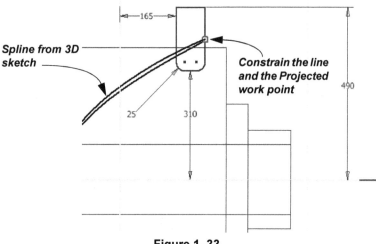

Spline from 3D sketch

Constrain the line and the Projected work point

Figure 1–33

6. In the Exit panel, click (Finish Sketch).

Task 4 - Create a swept cut.

1. Create a swept cut using the path and profile that have just been created. Return the model to the Shaded view display. The model displays as shown in Figure 1–34.

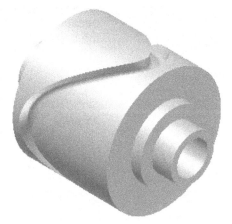

Figure 1–34

2. Add fillets of **10 mm** on the outside edges of the swept cut to remove sharp edges. Return the model to its shaded display. The model displays as shown in Figure 1–35.

Figure 1–35

3. Save and close the model.

Practice 1b | Imported Point Data

Practice Objectives

- Create a 2D and 3D sketch that reads points from a Microsoft Excel spreadsheet file.
- Set the options for imported points in a 3D sketch to import points only, import the points with connecting lines, or import points with a connecting spline.
- Create a swept extrusion that references a sketched profile and a 3D sketched path.

In this practice, you will import point data to create both 3D and 2D sketches. Using this data, you will then create the swept geometry shown in Figure 1–36.

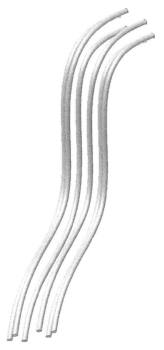

Figure 1–36

Task 1 - Create a 3D sketch.

The 3D sketch can be sketched using the tools in the Draw panel, or you can import point data. In this task, you will import point data using a few different methods.

1. Create a new part file with the standard English template, **Standard (in).ipt**.

2. In the *3D Model* tab>Sketch panel, click  (Start 3D Sketch). The *3D Sketch* tab is now the active tab.

3. In the Insert Panel, click (Points).

4. Select **chute_path.xls** and click **Open**. The spreadsheet was created for this practice and contains the X, Y, and Z coordinates for six points, as shown in Figure 1–37. Figure 1–37 shows the points in the default Home view.

Figure 1–37

5. In the Model browser, expand **Origin** and place the cursor over the Center Point work feature. Note that the Center Point and one of the imported points are coincident. Imported points reference the sketch origin (Center Point).

6. In the Draw panel, click (Line).

7. Right-click in the graphics window and verify that **Auto Blend** is disabled in the shortcut menu.

8. Reorient the model so that it is in the Home view, if not already. Starting from the top most point (sketch origin), select each point to draw lines between each of them, as shown in Figure 1–38. Right-click and select **OK**.

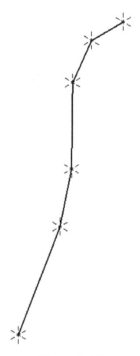

Figure 1–38

The line joining the points is not smooth. To smooth out the line, you can delete linear entities, add arcs, and assign tangency; however, doing so will change the point locations. Depending on your design intent, this might be acceptable, but for this design the points must remain as originally assigned.

9. Select all points and entities, and then delete them from the sketch.

10. In the *Tools* tab>Options panel, click (Application Options). In the Application Options dialog box, select the *Sketch* tab and enable **Auto-bend with 3D line creation** at the bottom of the window. Close the dialog box.

11. Select the *3D Sketch* tab.

12. In the Insert Panel, click ⊞ (Points).

13. Select **chute_path.xls** and click **Options**.

14. Select **Create lines** and click **OK** in the File Open Options dialog box. This dialog box enables you to control how the points are brought into the sketch. The default option only brings in the points from the file.

15. Click **Open** to bring the points into the sketch. Note that the points have been added and lines have been drawn for you. In addition, because **Auto Blend** was enabled, the curve is smoother. The data displays as shown in Figure 1–39.

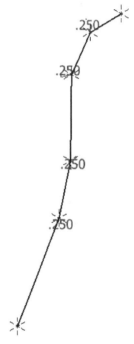

Figure 1–39

16. Select all points and entities, and then delete them from the sketch.

17. In the Insert Panel, click ⊞ (Points).

18. Select **chute_path.xls** and click **Options**.

19. Select **Create spline** and click **OK** in the File Open Options dialog box.

20. Click **Open** to bring the points into the sketch as a spline. The data displays as shown in Figure 1–40.

Figure 1–40

21. In the Exit panel, click (Finish Sketch).

Depending on the design intent of your model, you can consider using any one of the three methods for importing point data and using it in the 3D sketch. For the remainder of this practice, you will use the data that was brought into the 3D sketch as a spline.

Task 2 - Create a 2D sketch.

1. In the *3D Model* tab>Sketch panel, click 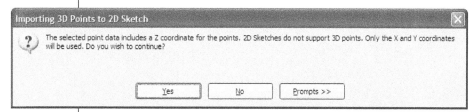 (Start 2D Sketch). Select the XY plane as the sketch plane. The *Sketch* tab is now the active tab.

2. In the Insert Panel, click ⬚ (Points).

3. Select **chute_profile.xls**. Before importing the data, verify in the File Open Options dialog box that it will be brought in as points. Open the file.

4. Click **Yes** in the dialog box that opens, as shown in Figure 1–41. This message notes that although X, Y, and Z coordinates are in the file, only the X and Y coordinates will be used to import the data.

Importing 3D Points to 2D Sketch

The selected point data includes a Z coordinate for the points. 2D Sketches do not support 3D points. Only the X and Y coordinates will be used. Do you wish to continue?

| Yes | No | Prompts >> |

Figure 1–41

5. Reorient the model to the Front view and zoom in, as shown in Figure 1–42. Six new points have been imported.

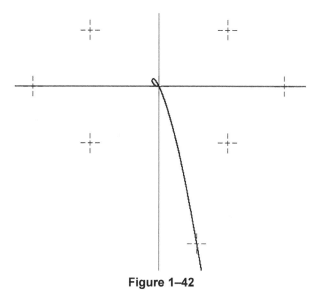

Figure 1–42

6. Sketch circular entities on all six points. Create a **.375** diameter dimension on one of the entities. Use the equal and fix constraints to locate the points where they have been imported. This ensures that all circular entities have the same diameter. The final sketch is shown in Figure 1–43.

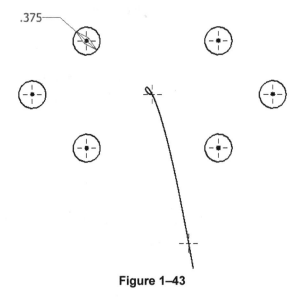

Figure 1–43

7. In the Exit panel, click ✔ (Finish Sketch).

Task 3 - Create swept geometry using the 2D and 3D sketches.

---

1. In the *3D Model* tab>Create panel, click 🍥 (Sweep).

2. Select the interior of one of the circular entities as a Profile for the sweep.

3. Disable the **Optimize for Single Selection** option. This enables you to select multiple references. Select the remaining circular entities (six total). If the **Optimize for Single Selection** option is enabled, you must manually enable the *Profile* reference selector to select each of the six profiles.

4. Once all six circular entities are selected as profiles, activate the 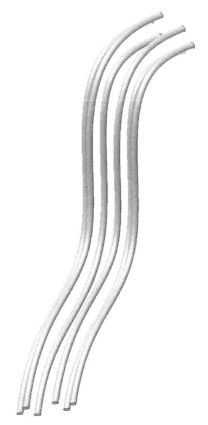 (Path) reference selector.

5. Select the 3D spline curve (imported in an earlier task) as the Path reference.

6. Complete the feature. The model displays as shown in Figure 1–44.

Figure 1–44

7. Save the model and close the window.

Chapter Review Questions

1. Which of the following correctly describes the difference between a 3D sketch and a 2D sketch? (Select all that apply.)

   a. In a 3D sketch there is no sketch plane.

   b. In a 3D sketch you use the **Fillet** command to add a bend between two linear entities.

   c. In a 3D sketch you have access to all of the same sketching constraints as those available in a 2D sketch.

   d. In a 3D sketch you can import points as can be done in a 2D sketch.

2. Which of the following describes how the **Include Geometry** option can be used in a 3D sketch?

   a. It enables you to copy sketched entities in a 3D sketch.

   b. It provides access to geometry creation options for creating 3D geometry using the 3D sketched entities.

   c. It enables you to reference existing entities in a model in a 3D sketch.

   d. It enables you to constrain entities in a 3D sketch.

3. Which 3D sketch tool can be used to create a curved entity that is defined by entering a formula for the x, y, and z axes?

   a. **Interpolation Spline**

   b. **Control Vertex Spline**

   c. **Equation Curve**

   d. **Bend**

4. You can create a 3D sketch curve from the intersection of two surfaces, work planes, or parts.

   a. True

   b. False

5. What are the three ways that imported point data can be brought into a 3D sketch?

   a. Points only

   b. Points with arcs connecting the points

   c. Points with lines connecting the points

   d. Points with a spline connecting the points

6. Which 3D sketch tool was used to create the entity shown in Figure 1–45?

Figure 1–45

   a. **Equation Curve**

   b. **Helical Curve**

   c. **Arc**

   d. **Control Vertex Spline**

   e. **Interpolation Spline**

7. Only the endpoints of a spline can be dimensioned in a sketch.

   a. True

   b. False

8. If a handlebar displays on a spline point, which type of spline was created?

   a. **Control Vertex Spline**

   b. **Interpolation Spline**

Answers: 1.(a,d), 2.c, 3.c, 4.a, 5.(a,c,d), 6.e, 7.b, 8.b

Command Summary

Button	Command	Location
N/A	3D Move/ Rotate (3D Sketch)	• **Context menu:** In the graphics window
	Arc Center Point (3D Sketch)	• **Ribbon:** *3D Sketch* tab>Draw panel
	Arc Three Point (3D Sketch)	• **Ribbon:** *3D Sketch* tab>Draw panel • **Context menu:** In the graphics window
	Bend (3D Sketch)	• **Ribbon:** *3D Sketch* tab>Draw panel • **Context menu:** In the graphics window
	Create 3D Sketch	• **Ribbon:** *3D Model* tab>Sketch panel
N/A	Delete (3D Sketch entity)	• **Context menu:** In the graphics window
N/A	Edit 3D Sketch (3D Sketch)	• **Context menu:** In Model browser • **Context menu:** In the graphics window
	Equation Curve (3D Sketch)	• **Ribbon:** *3D Sketch* tab>Draw panel
	Helical Curve (3D Sketch)	• **Ribbon:** *3D Sketch* tab>Draw panel • **Context menu:** In the graphics window
	Include Geometry (3D Sketch)	• **Ribbon:** *3D Sketch* tab>Draw panel • **Context menu:** In the graphics window
	Intersection Curve (3D Sketch)	• **Ribbon:** *3D Sketch* tab>Draw panel
	Line (3D Sketch)	• **Ribbon:** *3D Sketch* tab>Draw panel • **Context menu:** In the graphics window
	Mirror (3D Sketch)	• **Ribbon:** *3D Sketch* tab>Pattern panel
	Point (3D Sketch)	• **Ribbon:** *3D Sketch* tab>Draw panel
	Points (3D Sketch)	• **Ribbon:** *3D Sketch* tab>Insert panel
	Project to Surface (3D Sketch)	• **Ribbon:** *3D Sketch* tab>Draw panel
N/A	Properties (3D Sketch)	• **Ribbon:** *3D Sketch* tab>Format panel • **Context menu:** In the graphics window

	Silhouette Curve (3D Sketch)	• **Ribbon:** *3D Sketch* tab>Draw panel
	Spline Control Vertex	• **Ribbon:** *Sketch* tab>Create panel • **Ribbon:** *3D Sketch* tab>Draw panel
	Spline Interpolation	• **Ribbon:** *Sketch* tab>Create panel • **Ribbon:** *3D Sketch* tab>Draw panel

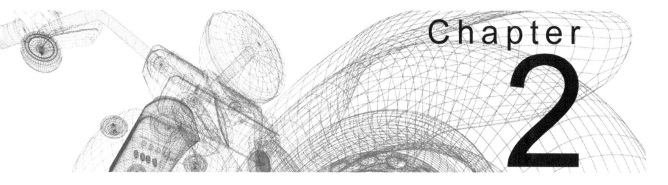

Introduction to Surfacing

The Autodesk® Inventor® software enables you to combine traditional surface modeling with advanced parametric modeling technology to create seamless, hybrid surface-solid models. Features such as an extrude, revolve, loft, or sweep can also be used to create surfaces or solids.

Learning Objectives in this Chapter

- Set the Surface Output type using the Feature dialog box or the mini-toolbar, so that features are created as surfaces.
- Create a planar surface by referencing a closed sketched profile.
- Create a three-dimensional surface that is defined by a series of planar and non-planar edges.
- Create a surface that is normal, tangent, or swept from reference entities to create surface geometry.
- Combine individual surface features into one quilted surface that can be used as a single surface for modeling.
- Add or remove material to a model by referencing a surface that defines the shape of the material to be added/removed.
- Create a surface that is offset by a specified amount from the face of a solid feature or another surface.
- Create solid geometry using surface geometry.
- Control whether a surface is displayed in a drawing views.

2.1 Introduction to Surfaces

A surface is a non-solid, zero-thickness feature that can define a contoured shape. Surfaces help capture the design intent of complex shapes that are not easily defined using solids. Surfaces can also be used as references to help create other features (solid and non-solid). The term "quilt" is often used to describe surface features and can refer to a single surface feature or a group of stitched (combined) surface features. Surface features can be used to do the following:

- Create surface models that can be converted to solid models.

- Create a "skin" over an imported wireframe model.

- Create complex solid cuts and extrusions.

- Create a solid form.

- Define complex curves.

A feature created using surfaces is shown in Figure 2–1.

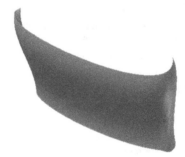

Figure 2–1

Surfaces display in the Model browser with symbols specific to their type, as shown in Figure 2–2. They are also listed in the **Surface Bodies** node at the top of the Model browser.

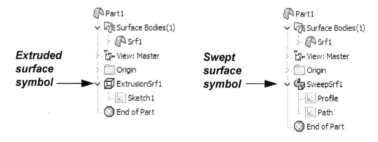

Figure 2–2

2.2 Basic Surfaces

When creating most features (such as extrudes, lofts, revolves, sweeps, and coils), you must select an *Output* type. This determines if the feature is created as a solid or a surface. To set the *Output* type as a surface, click 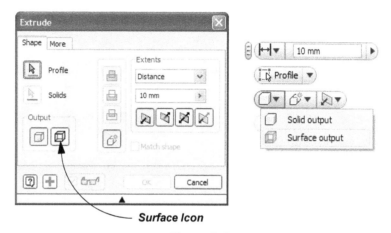 (Surface) in the feature dialog box or select **Surface output** in the mini-toolbar, as shown in Figure 2–3.

Surface Icon

Figure 2–3

- Creating a solid requires a closed profile, but a surface can be created using an open or closed profile. Defining the remaining options for a surface is the same as creating a solid feature and can be done using the dialog box or the mini-toolbar.

- All surfaces created in a part model are created as their own surface bodies, and are independently listed in the **Surface Bodies** node of the Model browser. Even if surfaces are combined, they create a new body in the list.

2.3 Patch Surfaces

Patch surfaces are surfaces created from closed 2D or 3D sketches, or existing closed boundary edges. Examples of a 2D and two 3D patch surfaces are shown in Figure 2–4.

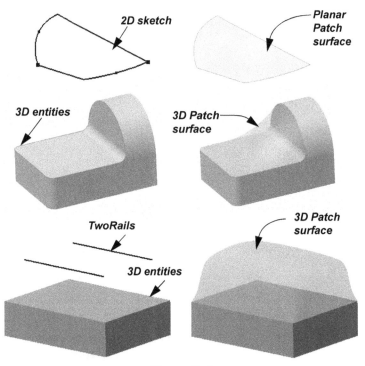

Figure 2–4

*When selecting the edges to form a patch, consider using **Automatic Edge Chain** to select adjacent edges together instead of individually selecting them.*

How To: Create Patch Surface

1. In the *Surface* panel, click ⬚ (Patch). The Boundary Patch dialog box opens.
2. Select a closed 2D or 3D sketch, or select edges on existing objects to form a closed profile.
3. (Optional) If edges are selected, you can also assign a boundary condition (i.e., Free, Tangent, Curvature Continuous, or G2) to the edge and its adjacent surfaces in the *Condition* area.
4. To further refine the shape of the patch surface, click

   ⬚ (Guide Rails) and select curves or points to drive the shape of the patch.
5. Click **OK** to create the surface.

- Surface patches are identified by the ⬚ symbol in the Model browser.

2.4 Ruled Surfaces

The **Ruled Surface** option enables you to create normal, tangent, and swept surfaces. A ruled surface is a surface where a straight line lies at every point on the surface. Common uses for this type of surface includes creating parting surfaces for mold design, creating surfaces that can split a body, or adding pockets.

How To: Create a Ruled Surface

1. Click ![icon](Ruled Surface) to open the Ruled Surface dialog box, as shown in Figure 2–5.

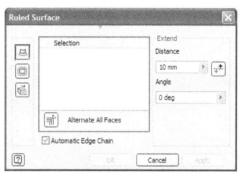

Figure 2–5

2. On the left-hand side of the dialog box, select the type of ruled surface.

   The dialog box options vary depending on the type of ruled surface you select.

   - Click (Normal) to create a ruled surface that remains normal along the edge reference.

   - Click (Tangent) to create a ruled surface that remains tangent along the edge reference.

   - Click (Sweep) to create a ruled surface that follows a direction vector along the edge reference.

3. Define references to create the ruled surface.
   - For Tangent or Normal ruled surfaces, select an edge reference to create the surface. Multiple edges can be selected. The references are listed in the *Edges Selection* area.

   *For Tangent and Normal ruled surfaces, select **Automatic Edge Chain** so that when selecting an edge, any edge that is tangent to it is also selected. Clear this option to select individual edges.*

   - For Sweep ruled surfaces, select an edge or sketch to define the path and a vector to define the direction. The direction vector can be a face, edge, or axis. If a sketch is being used, it must already exist in the model.

4. Enter a value in the *Distance* field to extend the edge(s) or sketch.

- Select 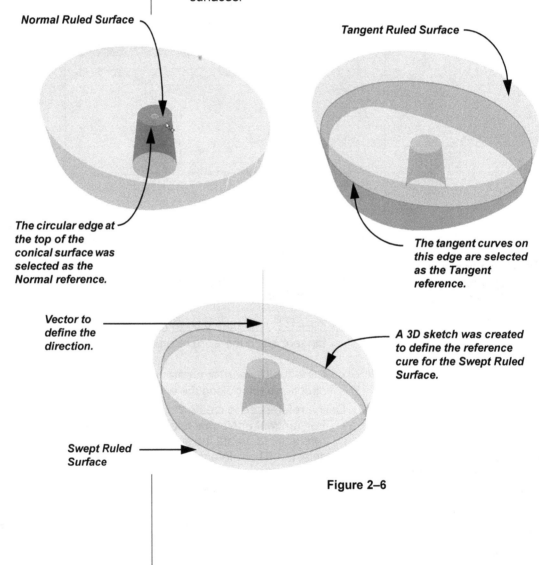 (Flip) to reverse the extension direction.

- Select (Alternate All Faces) to reverse the faces that are being used to define the directions.

5. (Optional) Enter an *Angle* value for the ruled surface.

6. Click **OK** to complete the ruled surface.

Figure 2–6 shows examples of the three types of ruled surfaces.

Normal Ruled Surface

Tangent Ruled Surface

The circular edge at the top of the conical surface was selected as the Normal reference.

The tangent curves on this edge are selected as the Tangent reference.

Vector to define the direction.

A 3D sketch was created to define the reference cure for the Swept Ruled Surface.

Swept Ruled Surface

Figure 2–6

2.5 Stitch Surfaces

A Stitch surface combines individual surface features into one surface feature. This option is useful when you want to split a part or surface, solidify a group of enclosed surfaces, or replace a face with a single item. When you stitch a group of surfaces together, you form a quilt. The quilt can be converted to a solid if it forms a closed volume.

How To: Stitch Surfaces to Form a Quilt

1. In the Surface panel, click ![Stitch icon] (Stitch) to create a quilt. The Stitch dialog box opens as shown in Figure 2–7.

Figure 2–7

2. Select the surfaces to create a quilt. The edges you are stitching must be the same size and adjacent to each other.
3. Click **Apply** to apply the feature. Continue stitching surfaces together or click **Done** to finish.

- Stitched quilts are listed in the Model browser, as shown in Figure 2–8 and a surface is added to the **Surface Bodies** node.

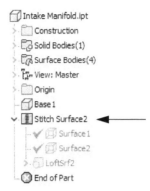

Figure 2–8

- To edit a stitched (quilt) surface, right-click it and select **Edit Feature**. When editing, you can add more surfaces to form larger quilts.

2.6 Sculpting with Surfaces

Sculpt can be used to add or remove material from a solid body using surfaces and work planes. Use Sculpt to create complex or stylized solid shapes that would be difficult to create using solid features. The selected surfaces and work planes, along with all the automatically selected solid faces of the model, are used to create a fully enclosed boundary that defines the solid volume to be added or removed.

Unlike the split and stitch options, sculpt surface references do not need to be trimmed.

How To: Add or Remove Material Using Sculpt

1. In the Surface panel, click ⬚ (Sculpt). The Sculpt dialog box opens, as shown in Figure 2–9.

Figure 2–9

2. Click ⬚ (Add) or ⬚ (Remove).
3. If material is added as a result of the sculpt, you can click

   ⬚ to create a new solid body from the resulting sculpted geometry.
4. Select the surfaces and work planes to form the boundary to add or remove. An example where one surface is selected and two solid faces are automatically selected is shown in Figure 2–10.

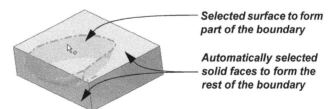

Selected surface to form part of the boundary

Automatically selected solid faces to form the rest of the boundary

Figure 2–10

5. Define the direction, as required, by clicking  and using the direction drop-down list for each individual surface, as shown in Figure 2–11. When adding material, the arrow highlighted in green shows what will be added. When removing material, the portion highlighted in red is what will be removed.

Figure 2–11

6. Click **OK** to complete the feature. An example of material removed using the sculpt feature is shown in Figure 2–12.

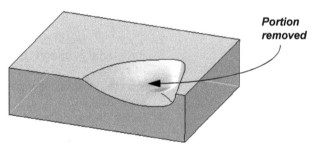

Portion removed

Figure 2–12

2.7 Thickening & Offsetting a Surface

Thickening and offsetting enables you to change the thickness of a part or surface or create offset surfaces from part faces or other surfaces. If you add thickness to a surface, it will become a solid. This option works only in the part environment. Surfaces in the construction environment cannot be thickened or offset. An offset surface created from a solid feature face and then thickened is shown in Figure 2–13.

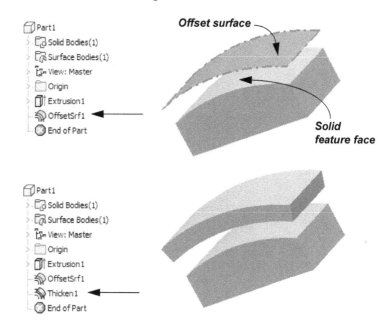

Figure 2–13

How To: Thicken/Offset a Surface Feature

1. In the Surface panel, click ⬦ (Thicken/Offset) to change the thickness of a part or surface, or to create offset surfaces from part faces or other surfaces.
2. Set **Automatic Blending**, if required.
    -   This option enables the blending of features when a solid face is selected. As the feature was thickened, this option blends the feature with any other interfering feature.
    -   If the **Automatic Blending** option is cleared, you can select to **Join**, **Cut**, or **Intersect** the thickened face with the model.

*If a surface feature is selected to be thickened, **Automatic Blending** becomes unavailable.*

3. Define the options on the *Thicken/Offset* tab, as shown in Figure 2–14:

   - Select the reference surface (**Quilt**) or face (**Face**).
   - Enter the offset distance.
   - Define whether the new feature is a solid or a surface.
   - Define whether material is added or removed.
   - Define the direction that the new feature is created.

   - If the resulting feature is a solid, you can click  to create a new solid body from the resulting thickened geometry.

Figure 2–14

4. Select the *More* tab. The options display as shown in Figure 2–15.

Figure 2–15

Option	Description
Automatic Face Chain	Automatically selects surfaces adjacent and tangent to the selected surface. This should be selected before selecting the face.
Create Vertical Surfaces	Enables you to create additional surfaces between the original and new surfaces on the edges between surfaces (not on outside edges).
Allow Approximation	Enables the system to deviate from the specified thickness when creating the surface. This can be used when a precise solution does not exist. If enabled you can select from **Mean** deviation, **Never too thin**, and **Never too thick**. Mean divides the thickness to fall both above and below the specified distance. Never too thin preserves the minimum distance. Never too thick preserves the maximum distance.
Optimized and **Specify Tolerance**	Affect the computation time when approximating a thickening. Optimized minimizes computation time by using a reasonable tolerance. Specify tolerance takes more time and uses a specified tolerance.

5. Click **OK** to complete the operation.

2.8 Surfaces in Drawing Views

Surfaces can be included or excluded from drawing views. You can set drawing views to include any type of surface, except for construction surfaces. All surfaces are automatically included in a view. Consider the following:

- Individual surfaces can be excluded from the view's display.

- If a surface is added and is visible in the model, the drawing view updates to reflect the display of the new surface.

- If a surface is deleted from the model, the drawing view is updated.

- If you want to include a construction surface, you must promote it to the Part environment before including it in a drawing view.

- Surfaces included in a Repaired Geometry node appear in a drawing view.

Include Surfaces

Included surfaces are visible in the drawing view. To include an individual surface in a view, expand the view containing the surface in the Model browser. In the **Surface Bodies** node, right-click on the required surface and select **Visibility**, as shown in Figure 2–16. By default, if the surface is displayed (visible) in the model, it will also display in the drawing view.

Figure 2–16

To include all surfaces that exist in a part, in the Model browser, expand the view to be modified. Right-click on the required part and select **Include All Surfaces**, as shown in Figure 2–17.

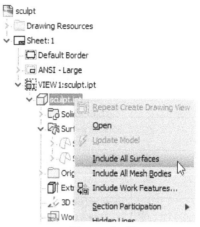

Figure 2–17

Exclude Surfaces

Excluded surfaces are hidden from the drawing view. To exclude a surface from a view, in the Model Browser, expand the view containing the surface. Right-click on the required surface in the **Surface Bodies** node and clear the checkmark beside **Visibility**. To exclude all surfaces contained in a part, clear the **Include All Surfaces** option. You can include and exclude surfaces in an assembly view in the same way as a part view.

Surfaces in Child Views

When a child view (such as a Projected or Auxiliary view) is created, it is generated based on the same surface display settings for the parent view. However, once it is created, including or excluding surfaces on a parent view does not have any effect on existing child views. Both views are independent in terms of the surface display settings.

For section and breakout views, hatching is only visible on solids, not surfaces.

Annotating Surfaces in a Drawing

You can modify surface edge properties, such as line type, line weight, and color. Right-click on the surface or on the surface edge and select **Properties**. The Edge Properties dialog box opens as shown in Figure 2–18.

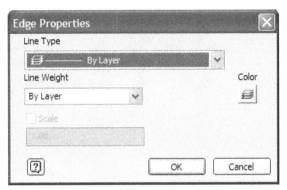

Figure 2–18

Annotations can be applied to surface edges once a surface is included in a view.

Practice 2a

Creating a Surface I

Practice Objectives

- Create an extruded surface for use as the termination plane for a solid cut.
- Mirror, fillet, and shell the geometry to achieve the required results.

In this practice, you will create a surface and use it to define an extruded cut on a bottle. You will also fillet and mirror the extruded cut and finally shell the bottle part. The resulting model is shown in Figure 2–19.

Figure 2–19

Task 1 - Create the extrusion.

In this task, you use the unconsumed sketch (**Sketch3**) to create a surface extrusion. Later in this practice, you use this surface as a termination plane for a solid cut.

1. Open **surface.ipt**.

2. The model contains **Sketch3**, an unconsumed sketch. Zoom and rotate as required to view this sketch.

3. Change the display mode to Wireframe display so that you can see the portion of the sketch inside the part, or hover over **Sketch3** in the Model browser to display it.

4. Start the **Extrude** option and click [] (Surface) as the *Output* type option. The *Output* type can be specified in the Extrude dialog box or in the mini-toolbar.

5. Select **Sketch3** as the profile and set the distance to **101.6 mm**, using either the Extrude dialog box or the mini-toolbar. Extrude symmetrically on each side of the sketch plane.

6. Complete the feature. The model displays as shown in Figure 2–20.

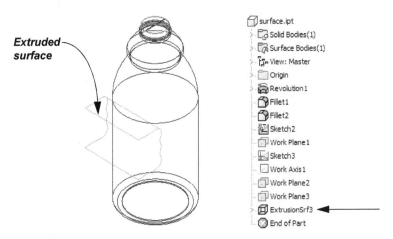

Extruded surface

Figure 2–20

Task 2 - Sketch the cut profile and create the cut.

1. Create a sketch on Work Plane3. Sketch and dimension the geometry shown in Figure 2–21. The location of the outside vertical lines are symmetric about the Work Axis1.

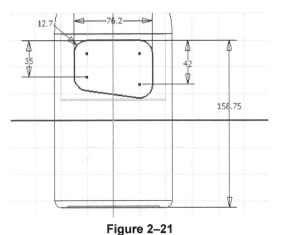

Figure 2–21

2. Start **Extrude** and click 🗔 to create a solid.

3. Select the new sketch as the profile. Using either the Extrude dialog box or the mini-toolbar, create the feature as a cut and set it to cut through to the surface feature.

4. In the Extrude dialog box, select the *More* tab and set the Taper angle to -**30 degrees**.

5. Complete the feature. Toggle off any visible work features and the surface. The model displays as shown in Figure 2–22.

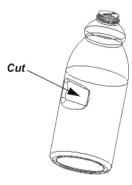

Figure 2–22

6. Fillet the inside edge of the cutout with a radius of **3.175mm**.

7. Mirror the features (surface extrusion, cut, and fillet) about the XY plane.

8. The mirrored surface is created as its own surface body. In the Model browser, expand the **Surface Bodies** node, right-click on **Srf2**, and clear the **Visibility** option.

9. Shell the bottle with a *Thickness* of **5 mm** removing the top face of the bottle. The shaded model displays as shown in Figure 2–23.

Figure 2–23

10. Save and close the model.

Practice 2b | Creating a Surface II

Practice Objectives

- Create a lofted surface that transitions between the edges on two alternate surfaces.
- Stitch the resulting lofted surface to the existing surfaces in the model to create a single surface and form a quilt.
- Create solid geometry from the stitched geometry using the Thicken/Offset command.

In this practice, you will create the portion of the model shown in Figure 2–24 by creating a Loft surface, stitching it together with two adjacent surfaces and finally thickening this surface to create solid geometry.

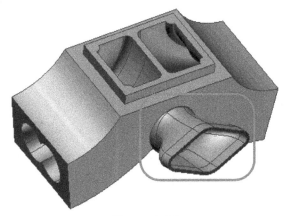

Figure 2–24

Task 1 - Create a loft surface.

1. Open **Intake Manifold.ipt**. You should see two surfaces listed in the **Surface Bodies** node of the Model browser. You will create a loft between these surfaces.

2. Start the creation of a loft. The Loft dialog box opens.

3. In the Loft dialog box, in the *Output* area, click ▣ (Surface) to create a surface.

4. In the *Sections* area, click **Click to add**.

5. Select the circular surface's edge. You might need to enable **Edge Chains** in the shortcut menu.

6. In the *Sections* area, click **Click to add** again and select the edge on the other surface, as shown in Figure 2–25.

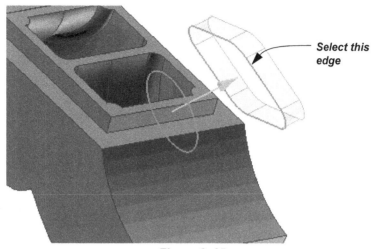

Figure 2–25

7. Select the *Conditions* tab.

8. Change both conditions from free to tangent, as shown in Figure 2–26.

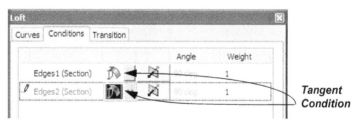

Figure 2–26

9. Click **OK** to complete the loft definition. The loft surface displays as shown in Figure 2–27.

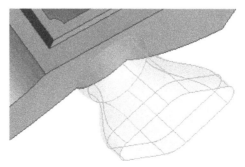

Figure 2–27

Task 2 - Stitch surfaces together.

1. In the Surface panel, click ⊞ (Stitch). The Stitch dialog box opens.

2. Select the Loft surface and its two adjacent surfaces, as shown in Figure 2–28.

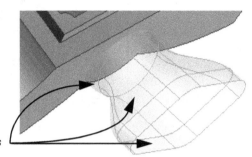

Select these three surfaces

Figure 2–28

3. Click **Apply** and **Done**. In the Model browser, in the **Surface Bodies** node, a fourth surface is added.

Task 3 - Use the Thicken/Offset option.

1. In the Modify panel, click ◇ (Thicken/Offset). The Thicken/Offset dialog box displays.

2. Select **Quilt** to easily select the stitched surface.

3. Select the stitched surface and set the *Distance* to **2 mm**.

4. Click **OK**. Toggle off visibility for the stitched surface. The model displays as shown in Figure 2–29.

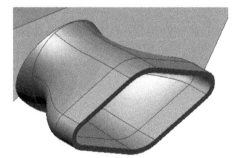

Figure 2–29

5. Save the part and close the window.

Practice 2c | Sculpting a Surface

Practice Objectives

- Add material to the model by referencing a surface that defines the shape of the material to be added.
- Remove material from the model by referencing a surface that defines the shape of the material to be removed.

In this practice, you use a sculpt feature to add and remove material, as shown in Figure 2–30.

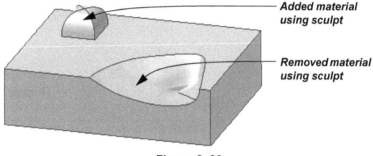

Added material using sculpt

Removed material using sculpt

Figure 2–30

Task 1 - Add material using the sculpt option.

1. Open **sculpt.ipt**.

2. Toggle on the visibility of the surface called **Add surface**. The surface displays as shown in Figure 2–31.

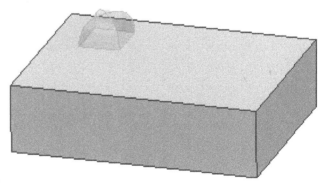

Figure 2–31

3. In the Surface panel, click ⬚ (Sculpt).

4. Select the surface called **Add surface**.

5. Click **OK** to complete the feature. The model displays as shown in Figure 2–32. The material in the Add surface feature has been added to the model. Once the feature is complete, note that the Add surface feature has automatically had its visibility removed.

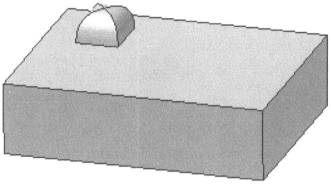

Figure 2–32

Task 2 - Remove material using the sculpt option.

1. Toggle on the visibility of the surface called Remove surface. The surface displays as shown in Figure 2–33.

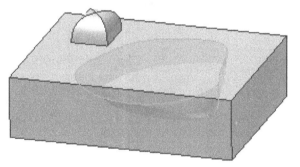

Figure 2–33

2. In the Surface panel, click ⬡ (Sculpt).

3. Click 🖶 (Remove).

4. Select the surface called Remove surface.

5. Click 〉〉 to expand the dialog box, as shown in Figure 2–34.

Figure 2–34

6. Select the direction column to access the drop-down list that defines the side of material to be removed. The portion to be removed is highlighted in red. Verify the side containing the smaller portion of material is removed, as shown in Figure 2–35.

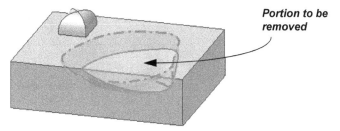

Portion to be removed

Figure 2–35

7. Click **OK**. The model displays as shown in Figure 2–36.

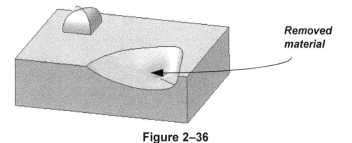

Removed material

Figure 2–36

8. Save and close the model.

Practice 2d

Ruled Surface Creation

Practice Objective

- Create normal, tangent, and swept ruled surfaces.

In this practice, you will learn how to use the **Ruled Surface** command to create normal, tangent, and swept ruled surfaces to complete a model. To complete the practice you will use the **Stitch** and **Thicken** commands to create solid geometry from surface geometry. The completed geometry is shown (in a top and bottom view) in Figure 2–37.

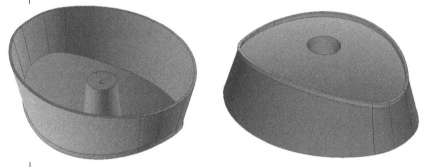

Figure 2–37

Task 1 - Create a ruled surface using the Normal type.

1. Open **Ruled_Surface.ipt** from the practice files folder.

2. In the *3D Model* tab>Surface panel, click (Ruled Surface). The Ruled Surface dialog box opens, as shown in Figure 2–38.

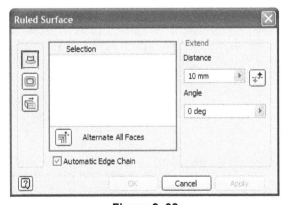

Figure 2–38

*The **Shaded with Edges** Visual Style setting was assigned to improve the clarity of the images.*

3. In the Ruled Surface dialog box, ensure that ⬚ (Normal) is selected, if not already set.

4. Select the circular edge, as shown in Figure 2–39.

5. Set the *Distance* to **10 mm**, if not already set as the default value. The surface that is previewed should be pointing toward the center of selected circle, as shown in Figure 2–39.

   If not, flip the orientation using the ⬚ button.

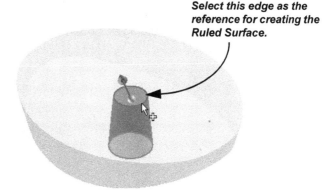

Select this edge as the reference for creating the Ruled Surface.

Figure 2–39

6. Click **Apply** to create the surface and leave the dialog box open to create additional surfaces.

7. In the Top view, zoom in on the surface. Note that the new ruled surface is perpendicular to the conical surface that is adjacent to it, not parallel to the bottom of the model. Figure 2–40 shows a sectioned view through the XY plane to visualize the ruled surface.

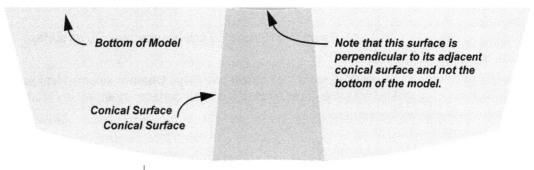

Bottom of Model

Note that this surface is perpendicular to its adjacent conical surface and not the bottom of the model.

Conical Surface
Conical Surface

Figure 2–40

Task 2 - Create a ruled surface using the Tangent type.

1. With the Ruled Surface command still active, in the Rule Surface dialog box, select ▣ (Tangent).

2. Set the *Distance* to **25 mm** and ensure that **Automatic Edge Chain** is selected.

3. Select the edge shown in Figure 2–41.

4. The preview of the tangent ruled surface displays, as shown in Figure 2–41. Click **Apply** to create the surface. Leave the dialog box open to create additional surfaces.

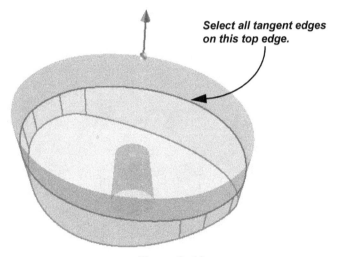

Select all tangent edges on this top edge.

Figure 2–41

Task 3 - Create a ruled surface using the Sweep type.

1. Select ▣ (Sweep) to activate the swept ruled surface option.

2. Ensure that **Automatic Edge Chain** is selected and select the lower edge of the outer surface, as shown in Figure 2–42.

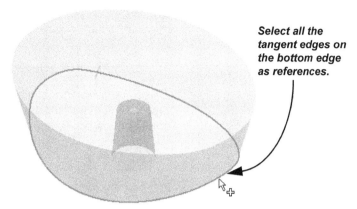

Select all the tangent edges on the bottom edge as references.

Figure 2–42

3. Select 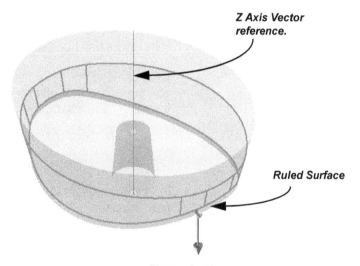 (Vector), if not already active. Expand the origin folder and select the **Z Axis** as the sweep direction vector.

4. Set the *Distance* to **5 mm** and flip the surface creation direction, if required. A preview of the swept ruled surface displays, as shown in Figure 2–43.

Z Axis Vector reference.

Ruled Surface

Figure 2–43

5. Click **OK** to create the surface.

Task 4 - Thicken the surfaces to create a solid part.

1. In the *3D Model* tab>Surface panel, click  (Stitch).

2. Select the five surfaces shown in Figure 2–44 to add to the new quilt. Do not select the swept ruled surface, as this causes the stitch to fail.

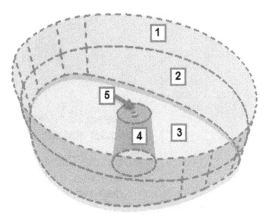

Figure 2–44

3. Click **Apply** to create the stitched surface quilt.

4. Click **Done** to complete the command. The surface updates and the edges between the tangent ruled surface and its selection have disappeared.

5. In the *3D Model* tab>Modify panel, click

   (Thicken/Offset).

6. In the Thicken/Offset dialog box select **Quilt** and select the newly created quilt.

7. Set the *Distance* to **2.5 mm**.

8. Flip the thicken direction, if required, so that the material is created to the inside of the part.

9. Click **OK** to thicken the part and create a new solid body.

10. Start the Thicken/Offset command again. Ensure that the

    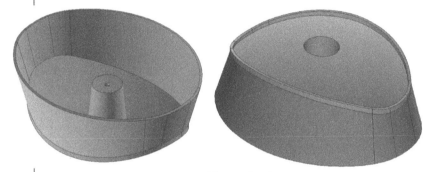 (Join) and **Quilt** selections are active and the *Distance* value remains at **2.5 mm**.

11. Select the swept ruled surface quilt. Flip the direction to create the solid geometry to the inside of the surface, if required.

12. Click **OK** to thicken the quilt and complete the command.

13. In the *View* tab>Visibility panel, expand the **Object Visibility** drop-down list and clear the **Construction Surfaces** selection.

14. Figure 2–45 shows the completed model from the top and bottom.

Figure 2–45

15. Save and close the part.

Chapter Review Questions

1. The thickness of an extruded surface can be entered in either the mini-toolbar or in the Extrude dialog box.

   a. True

   b. False

2. Which of the following statements is true regarding surface features? (Select all that apply.)

   a. The profile of the surface must be closed.

   b. Only a single surface body can exist in a model.

   c. When creating an extruded surface, **Join** and **Cut** options are not available.

   d. When creating an extruded surface, the depth extent options are the same as those for extruding a solid.

3. Which of the following options can be used to create a planar surface from a closed 2D sketch?

   a. Extrude

   b. Loft

   c. Stitch

   d. Sculpt

   e. Thicken/Offset

   f. Patch

4. Which of the following options can be used to add or remove solid material from a model by referencing a surface body? (Select all that apply.)

   a. Extrude

   b. Loft

   c. Stitch

   d. Sculpt

   e. Thicken/Offset

   f. Patch

5. The **Thicken/Offset** option enables you to add solid geometry to a model by referencing either a surface or solid face.

   a. True

   b. False

6. Which of the following options can be used to combine two or more surfaces together?

   a. Extrude

   b. Loft

   c. Stitch

   d. Sculpt

   e. Thicken/Offset

   f. Patch

7. Which of the following are valid Ruled Surface creation options? (Select all that apply.)

   a. Normal

   b. Tangent

   c. Loft

   d. Sweep

8. Which of the following best describes how excluding a surface in a drawing view affects its children views?

   a. When the visibility of a surface in a parent view is cleared, the visibility of that surface in all of its existing children views are updated to reflect the change.

   b. When the visibility of a surface in a parent view is cleared, the visibility of that surface in all of its existing children views do not change and the surface remains displayed.

Answers: 1.b, 2.(c,d), 3.f, 4.(d,e), 5.a, 6.c, 7.(a,b,d), 8.b

Command Summary

Button	Command	Location
N/A	Include all Surfaces	• **Context menu**: In Model Browser with model name selected
	Patch	• **Ribbon:** *3D Model* tab>Surface panel
N/A	Properties (edge Properties for surface in a drawing)	• **Context menu** with surface selected in the required view
	Ruled Surface	• **Ribbon:** *3D Model* tab>Surface panel
	Sculpt	• **Ribbon:** *3D Model* tab>Surface panel
	Stitch	• **Ribbon:** *3D Model* tab>Surface panel
	Thicken/ Offset	• **Ribbon:** *3D Model* tab>Modify panel

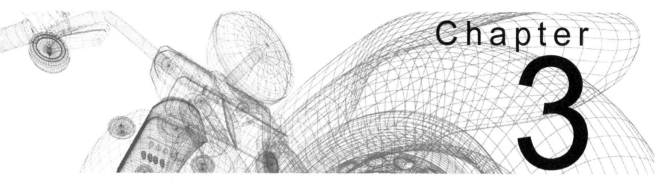

3

Additional Surfacing Options

There are a number of tools in the Autodesk® Inventor® software that enable you to manipulate surfaces that have been created in a model. Understanding these tools and how they can be used to obtain the required surface and solid geometry enables you to create robust models.

Learning Objectives in this Chapter

- Remove portions of a surface using a reference surface or work plane.
- Increase the extent of a surface by extending it at a selected edge so that the surface maintains the curve directions of the edges adjacent to the selected edge.
- Increase the extent of a surface by stretching it at a selected edge so that the surface remains normal to the edge.
- Create a new solid face by replacing an existing solid face with surface geometry.
- Remove existing surfaces or solid faces from the model to aid in surface modeling.
- Copy surfaces to a Repaired Geometry node so that they can be opened and manipulated in the Repair environment.
- Copy surfaces from one model into another in the context of an assembly.

3.1 Extend and Trim Surfaces

Trim Surface

The **Trim Surface** option enables you to trim an existing surface feature using another surface feature or work plane.

How To: Trim a Surface

1. In the *3D Model* tab>Surface panel, click ✂ (Trim).
2. Select geometry to represent the cutting tool. In Figure 3–1, the cutting tool represents another surface.

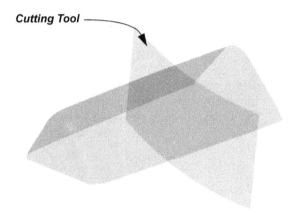

Cutting Tool ⎯⎯

Figure 3–1

3. Select the portion of the surface you want to remove, as shown in Figure 3–2. Once the portion to be removed is

   selected, it is highlighted in green. You can click 🔲 in the Trim Surface dialog box to invert the selection, if required.

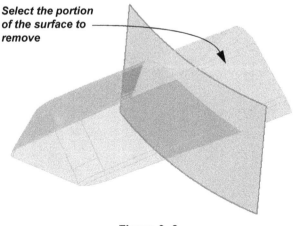

Select the portion of the surface to remove ⎯⎯

Figure 3–2

4. Click **OK** to complete the feature. Figure 3–3 shows the resulting surface after trimming.

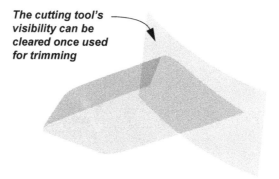

The cutting tool's visibility can be cleared once used for trimming

Figure 3–3

Extend Surface

Extend Surface enables you to increase the size of surfaces in one or more directions. You can specify a distance by which a surface is to increase or a termination face to which the surface is extended to.

How To: Extend a Surface

1. In the *3D Model* tab>Surface panel, click ⬆ (Extend). The Extend Surface dialog box opens as shown in Figure 3–4.

Figure 3–4

2. Select one or more edges to extend, as shown in Figure 3–5.

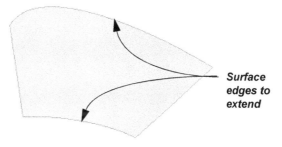

Surface edges to extend

Figure 3–5

3. Enter a distance or specify a termination reference.

4. Click >> to expand the dialog box. Select **Extend** to extend the selected edges along the same curve direction as the adjacent edges, as shown on the left side in Figure 3–6. Select **Stretch** to extend the selected edges in a straight line from the adjacent edges, as shown on the right side in Figure 3–6.

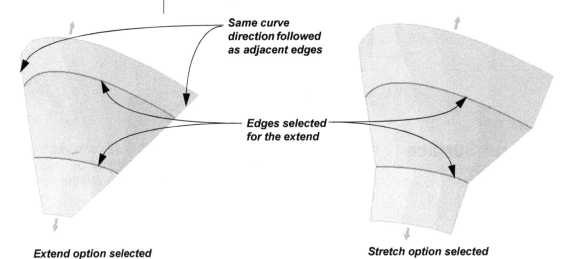

Same curve direction followed as adjacent edges

Edges selected for the extend

Extend option selected   *Stretch option selected*

Figure 3–6

5. Click **OK** to complete the feature.

3.2 Replace Face with a Surface

The **Replace Face** option enables you to replace any face of a part with another surface. This is useful for creating parts using simple surfaces. Figure 3–7 shows a face replaced with a surface on the right side.

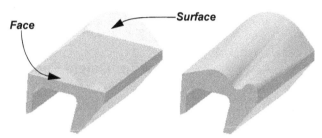

Figure 3–7

How To: Replace a Face with a Surface

When you replace a face with a face defined by a surface, you create a feature relationship between features. You can toggle off the visibility of the surface, but you cannot delete it. If you delete the surface, the new face is also deleted.

1. In the *3D Model* tab>Surface panel, click ⬚ (Replace Face). The Replace Face dialog box opens as shown in Figure 3–8.

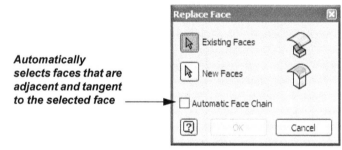

Figure 3–8

2. Select the existing part face that is to be replaced.

3. Click ⬚ (New Faces) and select the replacing surface. The new face must completely intersect the part face.

4. Click **OK** to complete the feature.

3.3 Delete Faces

The **Delete Face** option enables you to remove unwanted surfaces, solid pieces, and hollow areas from a model in the part environment. This is useful when doing hybrid solid/surface modeling. For instance, a loft operation may have created an unwanted "dent" in the object. You can clean it up by deleting the face(s), creating a new lofted surface with the required shape, then stitching everything back together to form a solid.

How To: Delete Faces

1. In the *3D Model* tab>Modify panel, click ⬜ₓ (Delete Face). The Delete dialog box opens as shown in Figure 3–9.

If a face on a solid is deleted, the solid becomes a surface.

Select a face

Heal option

Select lump or void (hollow area)

Figure 3–9

2. Select the faces to delete.

   - Use the 📦 (Select individual face) and 📦 (Select lump or void) icons to determine how faces are selected, either individually or select one face on a lump and have all faces in that lump selected.
   - A lump is a solid piece, such as a portion that remains after a Cut operation, that splits a part into multiple pieces. A void is a hollow area in a part.

*Healing can be valuable if you remove the face created by a chamfer. The **Heal** option extends the sides to restore the edge. This option is not available with Select lump or void.*

3. If required, select **Heal** when a face on a solid is deleted and you want the system to extend the adjacent faces to keep the part a solid.
4. Click **OK** to complete the feature.

3.4 Copy Surfaces

The Repair environment has options to repair surface geometry for use in the Part environment.

The **Copy Object** option can be used to transfer surfaces as follows:

- Copy a surface to a Repaired Geometry node so that it can be opened and manipulated in the Repair environment.

- Copy geometry in an assembly from one part to another part. You can then use the copied geometry as reference geometry to create new geometry.

How To: Copy Objects

1. If you are using **Copy Object** to copy information between components you must first assemble the components in a temporary assembly.
2. In the assembly, activate the component into which you will be copying the surface geometry.
3. In the *3D Model* tab>expanded Modify panel, click ⬚ (Copy Object) to copy surfaces to the Part environment. The Copy Object dialog box opens as shown in Figure 3–10.

Figure 3–10

4. Select the object to copy.
   - Select **Face** to select individual faces of a surface or surfaces of a solid.
   - Select **Body** to select entire surfaces or entire solids.

5. Select any additional options described below:

Create New		The **Create New Output** options depend on the selection of the face/body. Select one of the following options to copy/move surfaces or solids:
	Group (⬜)	Copies/moves the selected geometry as a new group in the Construction environment.
	Repaired Geometry (⬜)	Copies/moves the selected geometry as a Repaired Geometry body that can be used to access the Repair environment.
	Surface (⬜)	Copies/moves the selected geometry as base surface feature(s) in the part model.
	Composite (⬜)	Copies/moves the selected geometry as a single composite feature in the part model. This option is only available if two or more items are selected.
	Solid (⬜)	Copies/moves the selected geometry as a base feature in the part model. This option is only available when the copied geometry can form solid geometry.
Select Existing		Enables the selection of a target composite feature or group. Associative objects are added to associative composites. Non-Associative data is added to non-associative composites.
Associative (only in Assembly, between components & not for Solid output)		When enabled, establishes a relationship source and the target geometry. The ⟳ symbol displays adjacent to the created feature to indicate it is associative (adaptive). To break the link, right-click on the feature in the browser and select **Break Link**.
Delete Original		Deletes the original copied/moved geometry. This option is not available for copying between parts in Assembly mode. The **Delete Original** option does not delete parametric geometry.

6. Click **Apply** to copy a surface to the part environment. Surfaces that are copied are removed from the Repair environment and are placed into the Part environment area of the Model browser.
7. Click **OK** to close the Copy Object dialog box.

Practice 3a

Extending Surfaces

Practice Objectives

- Increase the extent of a surface by extending the surface at a selected edge, such that the extended surface maintains the curve directions of the edges adjacent to the selected edge.
- Increase the extent of a surface by stretching the surface at a selected edge, such that the stretched surface remains normal to the edge.

In this practice, you extend a surface using the two available extend options: **Extend** and **Stretch**, as shown in Figure 3–11.

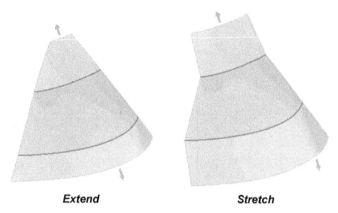

Extend   *Stretch*

Figure 3–11

Task 1 - Use the Extend Surface option.

1. Open **extend surface.ipt**.

2. In the *3D Model* tab>Surface panel, click ⬆ (Extend).

3. Verify that **Distance** is selected in the Extents drop-down list.

4. Reorient the model and select the edges shown in Figure 3–12.

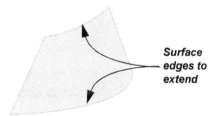

Surface edges to extend

Figure 3–12

5. Set the *Distance* to **15**.

6. Click >> to expand the dialog box. Verify that **Extend** is selected to extend the selected edges along the same curve direction as the adjacent edges. The preview displays as shown in Figure 3–13.

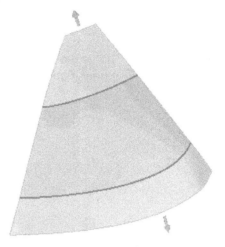

Figure 3–13

7. Select **Stretch** to extend the selected edges in a straight line from the adjacent edges, as shown in Figure 3–14.

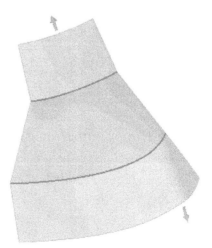

Figure 3–14

8. Click **OK** to complete the extend.

9. Save and close the model.

Practice 3b

Copying Surfaces

Practice Objectives

- Copy the geometry of one part model into another part model in the context of an assembly.
- Using copied surface geometry, replace an existing solid face with the copied surface geometry to create a new solid face.

In this practice, you copy a surface to another part in an assembly, and use the surface to replace a face on that part. The resulting component is shown in Figure 3–15.

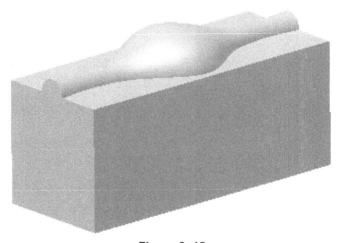

Figure 3–15

Task 1 - Create a new assembly file.

1. Create a new assembly file using the Metric template.

2. Place one instance of **blank.ipt**. Right-click and select **Place Grounded at Origin**. The first component in the assembly is grounded at the origin (0,0,0).

3. Place one instance of **shape.ipt**.

4. Show the assembly degrees of freedom (*View* tab>Visibility panel>click ⟳ (Degrees of Freedom)).

5. Fully constrain **shape.ipt** as shown in Figure 3–16. The model is displayed in wireframe.

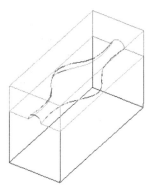

Figure 3–16

Task 2 - Copy shape.ipt.

1. Activate **blank.ipt** in the assembly.

2. In the *3D Model* tab>expanded Modify panel, click  (Copy Object) to copy *shape.ipt* into **blank.ipt**.

3. Select the shape component in the graphics window.

4. Click **Apply** to copy the shape component using the default options in the Copy Object dialog box. Only the

   (Composite) option should be selected.

5. Close the dialog box. The Model browser displays as shown in Figure 3–17.

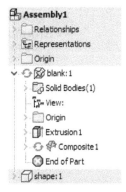

Figure 3–17

Task 3 - Replace the part face with the copied surface.

In this task, you open the blank component in a separate window and replace the blank component's top face with the copied surface.

1. Open **blank.ipt** in a separate window. The part displays as shown in Figure 3–18. Surfaces from **shape.ipt** have been added.

Figure 3–18

2. In the *3D Model* tab>Surface panel, click 🔼 (Replace Face) to replace a face in the part with the copied surface.

3. Select blank.ipt's top face as the existing face.

4. Click 🔲 (New Faces). Select the curved face and its two adjacent flat faces, as shown in Figure 3–19. Be sure to select all three faces.

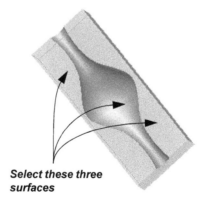

Select these three surfaces

Figure 3–19

5. Click **OK**. Toggle off the visibility of the copied surface (**Composite1**). The blank part displays as shown in Figure 3–20.

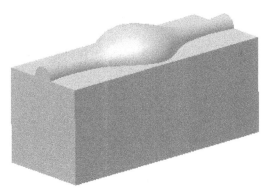

Figure 3–20

6. Save the part and assembly. If changes are made to shape.ipt, the assembly can be updated and the change will reflect in the **blank.ipt** component. If the assembly is not kept the associativity between the two components is lost and if changes are made to shape.ipt they are not reflected in **blank.ipt**.

7. Close the window.

Practice 3c

Deleting a Surface

Practice Objectives

- Combine adjacent surfaces to form a single quilted surface that can be easily selected as a reference when creating other features.
- Remove an existing surface from the model.
- Create a surface that is defined by a series of edges to create a three-dimensional surface.
- Create solid geometry from a surface using the Thicken/Offset command.

In this practice, you create a thicken feature using an imported surface. Based on the surface geometry, it cannot be created with the required thickness. To resolve the error you will delete the problem surface and create a new boundary surface. The resulting model, after a successful thicken feature is added, is shown in Figure 3–21.

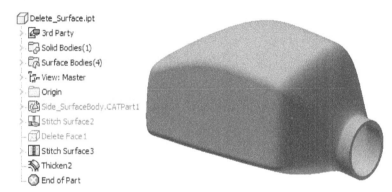

Figure 3–21

Task 1 - Open a part file.

1. Open **Delete_Surface.ipt**. Note that in the Model browser, a surface is listed in the **Surface Bodies** node. This surface has been imported from another CAD system.

Task 2 - Stitch surfaces together.

1. In the Surface panel, click ⬚ (Stitch). The Stitch dialog box opens.

2. Select the surface body, as shown in Figure 3–22. All of the surfaces in the body are selected.

Figure 3–22

3. Click **Apply** and **Done**. In the Model browser, in the **Surface Bodies** node, a second surface is added.

Task 3 - Use the Thicken/Offset command.

---

1. In the Modify panel, click (Thicken/Offset). The Thicken/Offset dialog box displays.

2. Select **Quilt** to easily select the stitched surface.

3. Select the stitched surface and enter a distance of **4 mm**.

4. Click **OK**. The Create Thicken feature dialog box opens indicating that the feature cannot be created due to the geometry. The 4 mm value is the minimum acceptable wall thickness for this model. A smaller value will work, however, will not meet the design requirement.

5. Click **Cancel** to close the dialog box.

Task 4 - Delete a face on the model.

To resolve the failure, you will delete a surface face from the imported geometry and then recreate a new surface that will accept the required wall thickness.

1. In the *3D Model* tab>expanded Modify panel, click

   ⬜× (Delete Face).

2. Verify that 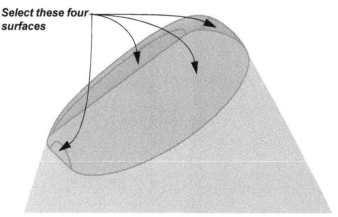 (Select Individual Face) is enabled.

3. Select the four faces as shown in Figure 3–23.

Select these four — *surfaces*

Figure 3–23

4. Click **OK**.

Task 5 - Create a boundary patch.

---

1. In the *3D Model* tab>Surface panel, click (Patch).

2. Select **Automatic Edge Chain** if it is not already selected. This enables you to select all the adjacent edges together instead of selecting them individually.

3. Select the circular edges bounding the face that was just deleted. A flat face immediately previews on the model, as shown in Figure 3–24.

Boundary Patch

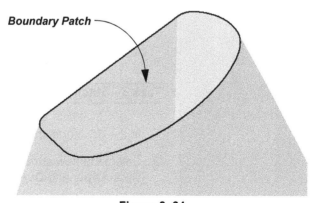

Figure 3–24

4. In the Boundary Patch dialog box, in the *Condition* area, in the selected edge drop-down list, click 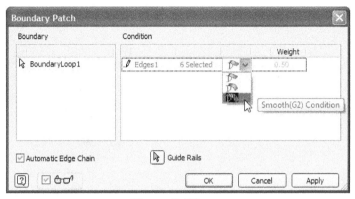 (Smooth G2), as shown in Figure 3–25, for the edges that defines the patch. This creates a smooth continuous condition between the patch and adjacent faces on the selected edge.

Figure 3–25

5. Maintain the default *Weight* value of **0.5**. Click **OK**. The model displays as shown in Figure 3–26.

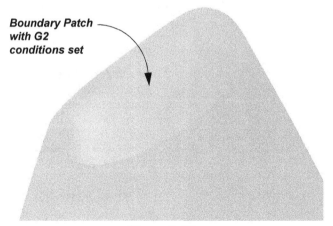

Boundary Patch with G2 conditions set

Figure 3–26

Task 6 - Stitch surfaces to create a solid.

1. In the *3D Model* tab>Surface panel, click ⊞ (Stitch).

2. Select the new surface and the existing stitched surface. Click **Apply** and **Done**.

Task 7 - Use the Thicken/Offset option.

1. In the Modify panel, click ⬭ (Thicken/Offset). The Thicken/Offset dialog box opens.

2. Select **Quilt** to easily select the stitched surface.

3. Select the stitched surface and set the *Distance* to **4 mm**.

4. Click **OK**. The solid geometry is created with a 4 mm thickness, as shown in Figure 3–27. By deleting the end portion of the surface geometry and simplifying it with the creation of a boundary patch that was G2 continuous with its adjacent surface, the geometry was able to be created.

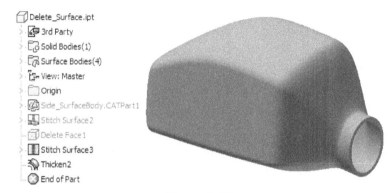

Figure 3–27

5. Save the model and close the window.

Practice 3d

Creating a Solid from Surfaces

Practice Objectives

- Trim a surface using another reference surface as the cutting tool.
- Remove an existing surface from the model.
- Create surfaces that are defined by a series of edges to create a three-dimensional surface.
- Create solid geometry by stitching surfaces together.

In this practice, you create solid geometry using imported surfaces as its foundation. Based on the surface geometry that is provided, you will trim it and create new surfaces to generate solid geometry. To complete the model you will shell it. After the solid has been created, the completed model will display as shown in Figure 3–28.

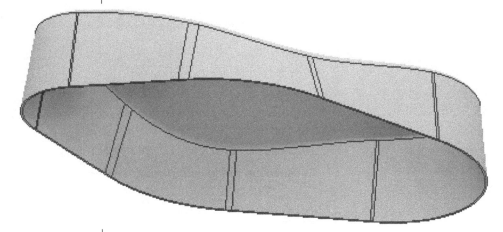

Figure 3–28

Task 1 - Trim a surface.

1. Open **Surface_to_Solid.ipt**. Note that in the Model browser, two surfaces are listed in the **Surface Bodies** node. These surfaces have been imported from another CAD system.

2. In the *3D Model* tab>Surface panel, click ✂ (Trim).

3. Select the Top surface as the cutting tool, as shown in Figure 3–29.

To invert the selection, in the Trim Surface dialog box, click 🔲↕, *as required.*

4. Select the portion of the surface you want to remove, as shown in Figure 3–29. Once the portion to be removed is selected, it is highlighted in green.

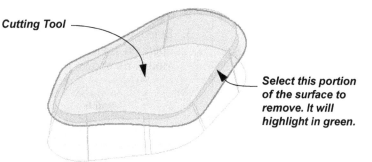

Cutting Tool

Select this portion of the surface to remove. It will highlight in green.

Figure 3–29

5. Click **OK** to trim the surface.

Task 2 - Delete a surface.

1. In the *3D Model* tab>Modify panel, click 🔲× (Delete Face).

2. Verify that 📖 (Select Individual Face) is enabled.

3. Select the surface shown in Figure 3–30 to delete.

In the Autodesk Inventor software, the edges of surfaces will display as yellow. The images in this practice show as black for the purposes of printing clarity.

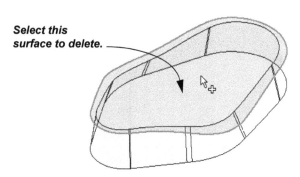

Select this surface to delete.

Figure 3–30

4. Click **OK** to delete the surface.

Task 3 - Create a boundary patch.

1. In the *3D Model* tab>Surface panel, click 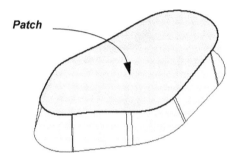 (Patch).

2. Ensure that **Automatic Edge Chain** is selected. This option enables you to select all of the adjacent edges together, instead of selecting them individually.

3. Select the chain of edges that were generated by the **Trim** option in Task 2. A flat face immediately previews on the model, as shown in Figure 3–31.

Patch

Figure 3–31

4. In the Boundary Patch dialog box, in the *Condition* area, in the Selected Edge drop-down list, click 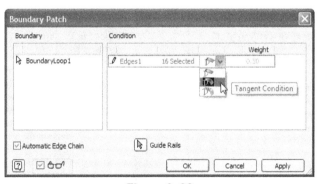 (Tangent Condition) (as shown in Figure 3–32) for the edges that define the patch. This creates a tangent condition between the patch and adjacent faces on the selected edge.

Figure 3–32

5. Set the *Weight* value to **0.2** to change the influence of tangency on the geometry. Reducing this value creates a flatter surface because tangency is maintained over a shorter distance. Click **OK**. The model appears as shown in Figure 3–33.

To further refine the shape of the boundary patch, a guide rail curve or a point can also be selected to control its shape.

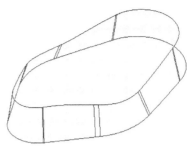

Figure 3–33

The remainder of the practice has you create a shelled solid from the imported and modified surfaces. Simply using the Thicken/Offset command does not provide for a flat lip on the bottom edge because a thickened solid remains normal to the surface, as shown in Figure 3–34. Alternatively, you will create an additional surface and then use it to create the solid geometry.

A surface is thickened normal to the reference surface and in this case does not create a flat lip.

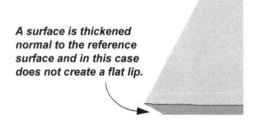

Figure 3–34

Task 4 - Create solid geometry from the surfaces.

1. In the *3D Model* tab>Surface panel, click ⬚ (Patch).

2. Select the edges along the Bottom surface, as shown in Figure 3–35.

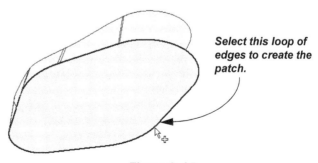

Select this loop of edges to create the patch.

Figure 3–35

3. Click **OK**.

4. In the Surface panel, click ⬚ (Stitch). The Stitch dialog box opens.

5. Select all three surfaces in the model by dragging a selection window around them. Maintain the default tolerance value and click **Apply**. The stitched surfaces form a watertight area, and therefore automatically generate a solid, as shown in Figure 3–36. Close the Stitch dialog box.

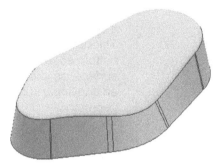

Figure 3–36

Task 5 - Add a shell to complete the solid geometry.

1. In the Modify panel, click ⬚ (Shell). The Shell dialog box opens.

2. Ensure that the shell is being created on the inside of the model.

3. Select the bottom flat surface as the surface to be removed.

4. Set the shell *Thickness* to **.125 in**.

5. Click **OK**. The solid geometry is created as shown in Figure 3–37.

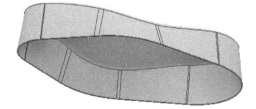

Figure 3–37

6. Save the model and close the window.

Practice 3e | Deleting a Face

Practice Objective

- Remove existing surfaces from the model so that the removed faces are automatically replaced by new surfaces.

In this practice, you will be provided a model (shown in Figure 3–38) that has been imported from another CAD system. In reviewing the model, you will note a design error and a geometry change that is required. Using the **Delete Face** option, you will fix these issues so that the geometry can be used.

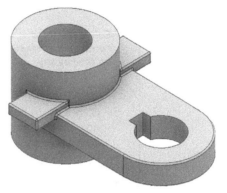

Figure 3–38

Task 1 - Delete faces on the model.

The keyway that is in the geometry is not required. The **Delete Face** option can be used to remove this.

1. Open **Delete_Face.ipt**. Note that in the Model browser, a single solid is listed in the **Solid Bodies** node and in the feature list. This solid has been imported from another CAD system.

2. In the *3D Model* tab>Modify panel, click ⬜ₓ (Delete Face).

3. Verify that ▥ (Select Individual Face) is enabled.

4. Select the three faces shown in the highlighted keyway in Figure 3–39.

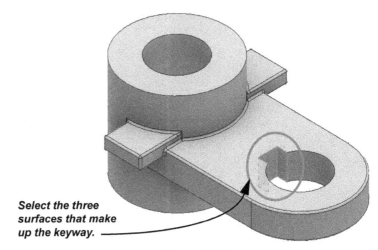

Select the three surfaces that make up the keyway.

Figure 3–39

5. Click **OK**. In the Model browser, note that the geometry is now listed in the **Surface Bodies** node. The removal of these faces has converted the solid model to surface geometry because it is no longer watertight.

To create a solid you could patch the openings with surface geometry and use **Sculpt** to create the solid. As an alternative, you will use a tool in the **Delete Face** command to heal the area where the faces were removed.

6. Double-click on the **Delete Face1** feature in the Model browser to edit the feature.

7. Select **Heal** in the Delete Face dialog box.

8. Click **OK**. Note how incorporating the use of the **Heal** option creates surfaces to replace those that are removed.

Task 2 - Delete additional faces on the inside of the model.

A modeling error was made in the original geometry and it must be corrected.

1. Rotate the model to view the hole shown in Figure 3–40. Note that there is a modeling error and that a rectangular extrusion exists in the hole.

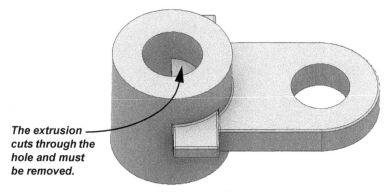

The extrusion cuts through the hole and must be removed.

Figure 3–40

2. Similar to the previous task, use the **Delete Face** command so that the three faces that must be removed are automatically healed. The final solid geometry should display as shown in Figure 3–41.

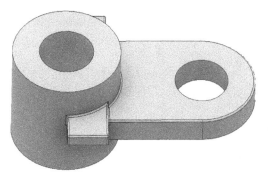

Figure 3–41

3. Save the model and close the window.

Chapter Review Questions

1. Which **Extend** surface option is used to extend the arc shown in Figure 3–42?

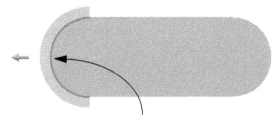

This edge of the surface was selected for extension

Figure 3–42

   a. Extend

   b. Stretch

2. Which option can be used to remove surface geometry on either side of an intersecting plane or surface?

   a. Trim

   b. Stitch

   c. Sculpt

   d. Patch

   e. Delete Face

   f. Replace Face

3. Which option can be used to edit existing geometry in a model with an intersecting surface?

   a. Trim

   b. Stitch

   c. Sculpt

   d. Patch

   e. Delete Face

   f. Replace Face

4. The **Delete Face** command can only be used to remove an existing surface in the model and not a solid face.

   a. True

   b. False

5. Which of the following statements are true regarding using the **Copy Object** option to copy surfaces between components? (Select all that apply.)

   a. To copy a surface between models, right-click on the surface in the source model and select **Copy Object**. Then open the new model, right-click, and select **Paste**.

   b. To copy surfaces between models, assemble them and use the **Copy Object** command in the target model.

   c. When using the **Copy Object** command you must use the **Face** command to select individual surfaces in the source model.

   d. Once a surface is copied between components. Changes to the original surface can never be reflected in the new model.

6. Match the command in the left column to its icon in the right column.

Command	Icon	Answer
a. Trim		_____
b. Extend		_____
c. Replace Face		_____
d. Delete Face		_____
e. Copy Object		_____

Answers: 1.b, 2.a, 3.f, 4.b, 5.(b,c), 6.(bedac)

Command Summary

Button	Command	Location
	Copy Object	• **Ribbon:** *3D Model* tab>expanded Modify panel
	Delete Face	• **Ribbon:** *3D Model* tab>Modify panel
	Extend (Surface)	• **Ribbon:** *3D Model* tab>Surface panel
	Replace Face	• **Ribbon:** *3D Model* tab>Surface panel
	Trim (Surface)	• **Ribbon:** *3D Model* tab>Surface panel

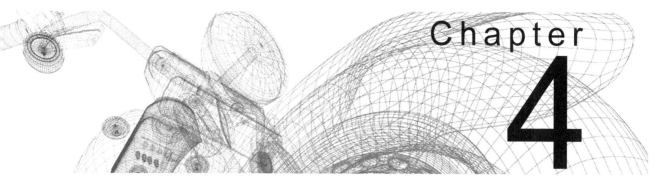

Introduction to Freeform Modeling

A Freeform Modeling workflow enables you to create complex, visually appealing shapes without the complex work that is required when using a Parametric Modeling workflow.

Learning Objectives in this Chapter

- Create freeform geometry base shapes, faces, and converted geometry.
- Edit freeform base geometry by manipulating existing geometry or adding new elements to the base shape.

4.1 Creating Freeform Geometry

Using conventional modeling techniques to create organic, highly shaped, and visually appealing models is often difficult and time-consuming. Freeform modeling is an alternate modeling approach for these types of surfaces. It enables you to create shapes that can be manipulated directly, without needing to use parametric constraints. These tools can be combined with parametric tools, where required.

Creating Standard Freeform Shapes

To begin the modeling process you must create the shape that is going to form the base geometry. Select the type that provides you with the best overall shape for the required geometry. The available shapes are shown in Figure 4–1.

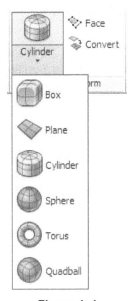

Figure 4–1

The overall procedure for creating the freeform shapes is similar and all of them use dialog boxes to define their geometry.

To create additional freeform shapes once in Freeform mode, select the geometry type from the Freeform tab> Create Freeform panel.

How To: Create a Base Freeform Shape

1. In the *3D Model* tab>Create Freeform panel, select the type of freeform shape to create. Figure 4–2 shows the dialog boxes that are used to create each shape type.

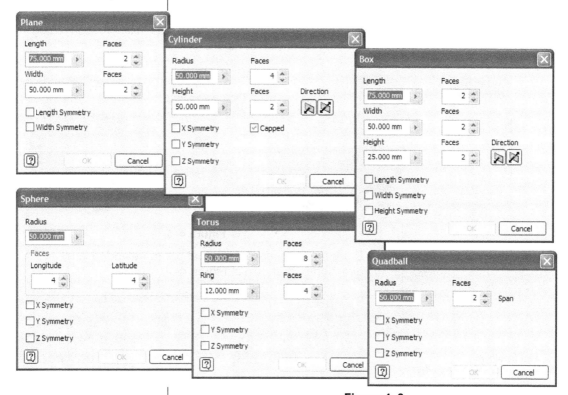

Figure 4–2

2. Select a work plane or planar face on which to place the freeform shape.
3. Select the center of the freeform shape.
   - Select the projected model origin to locate the shape at the origin center point.
   - If creating a freeform shape on an existing face, geometry points are projected from the model and can be selected as the center point reference.
   - If no reference point exists, you can also select anywhere on the plane.

4. Manipulate the size of the freeform shape using any of the following techniques:

- Drag the arrowheads that display on the model. The active arrowhead is displayed in gold. Select any of the other arrowheads to activate them for dragging. Figure 4–3 shows the default shape and arrowheads available for a Box and Cylinder.

- Enter values for the freeform size in its creation dialog box, as shown in Figure 4–3.

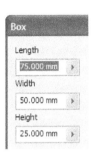

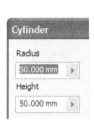

Figure 4–3

5. Enter the number of faces that are to be added in all directions, as shown in Figure 4–4.

The freeform shape is more refined when more faces are added. Note that using too many sides can create too much control.

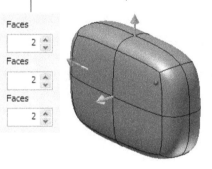

Figure 4–4

- For a Sphere freeform, you enter the number of faces in the longitudinal and latitudinal directions. For the Quadball freeform, only a single face field is provided.

6. Assign symmetry by selecting the appropriate axis/directions in the creation dialog box.

   - Hover the cursor over each option to display the symmetry plane that will be used.
   - Once assigned, black edges display as a dashed yellow edge to identify the symmetry lines.

Hint: Defining Symmetry

The symmetry that is assigned during base freeform creation cannot be removed from the model. If symmetry is required in the model, you can use ⬛ (Symmetry) in the Symmetry panel to explicitly assign symmetry between selected faces.

7. For the Box and Cylinder freeform shapes, select the direction in which the freeform shape is to be created relative to the placement plane by clicking ⬛ and ⬛.
8. Click **OK**.

Figure 4–5 shows the available shapes. Each have been manipulated using the options in their creation dialog boxes. The Model browser shown on the left is the same regardless of the type of shape created. It indicates that a **Form** feature has been added to the model.

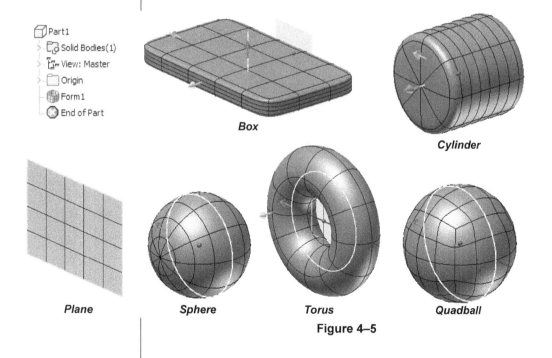

Box

Cylinder

Plane

Sphere

Torus

Quadball

Figure 4–5

Creating a Face Freeform

A **Face** Freeform enables you to create an irregular, planar, or non-planar face as the base freeform geometry. It can also be used to close a gap.

How To: Create a Face

1. In *3D Model* tab>Create Freeform panel, select ✤ (Face). The Face dialog box opens as shown in Figure 4–6.

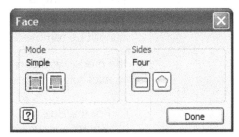

Figure 4–6

To create additional faces once you are in Freeform mode, select

✤ *(Face) from the Freeform tab> Create Freeform panel.*

2. Set how the face is to be created using the options in the *Mode* area:

   - Select ▣ (Point) to select individual points to define the face.

   - Select ▣ (Edge) to select an edge and two points to define the face.

By default, if points are selected individually without referencing existing entities, the points create a planar face.

3. Define the number of corners in the face in the *Sides* area:

   - Select ▢ (Four) to create a face with four boundary points.

   - Select ⬠ (Multiple) to create a face with any number of points. To complete the face, you must select the first selected point a second time.

4. Select points to define the face.
5. Click **Done** to complete the face.

Converting Geometry to a Freeform

Existing solid faces and surface 3D geometry can be converted into a freeform object using **Convert**. Once converted, it copies the shape of the original geometry and becomes freeform geometry, enabling you to use all of the editing tools to further manipulate the shape of the model.

How To: Convert to Freeform Geometry

To convert additional faces once in Freeform mode, select

(Convert) from the Freeform tab>Create Freeform panel.

1. In the *3D Model* tab>Create Freeform panel, click

    (Convert). The Convert to Freeform dialog box opens, as shown in Figure 4–7.

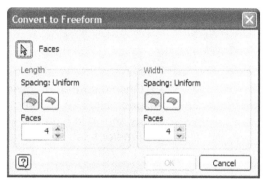

Figure 4–7

2. Select faces on a solid or surface model.
3. Define how the faces will be created in the converted freeform geometry for Length:

    •   Select (Uniform) to create the converted geometry with uniform spacing and enter the number of faces to be created.

    •   Select (Curvature) to create the converted geometry with curvature and enter a deviation value to define how it should be divided in the Length.

If the resulting shape is different from the original, increase the number of faces to more closely match it.

4. Set values in the *Width* area to define how the faces will be created in the converted freeform geometry. The available options are the same as in *Length*.
5. Click **OK** to complete the conversion to freeform geometry.

The solid geometry shown in Figure 4–8 was selected for conversion. Once converted, you can use the editing tools in the freeform environment to manipulate the shape, as required.

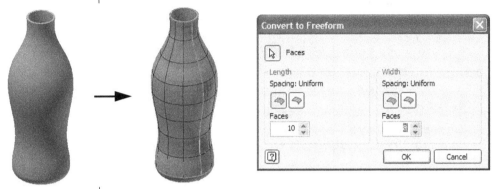

Figure 4–8

Once the freeform base solid, face, or converted freeform geometry has been created, the Freeform environment is active, as shown in Figure 4–9. All of the commands outside the *Freeform* tab are unavailable.

Figure 4–9

Hint: Toggle Smooth

Use the (Toggle Smooth) option located in the Tools panel to toggle the freeform from a smooth to blocky mode display type, as shown in Figure 4–10. When in Blocky mode, the performance is faster. The model is still smooth once it has been toggled off or when Freeform mode is off.

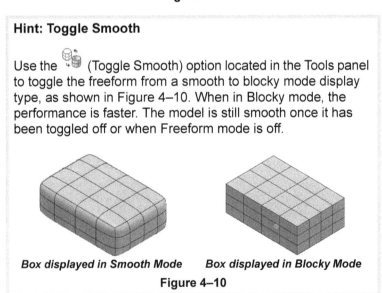

Box displayed in Smooth Mode   *Box displayed in Blocky Mode*

Figure 4–10

Deactivating and Activating Freeform Mode

To exit the Freeform environment, either:

- Click ✔ (Finish Freeform) in the Exit panel.

- Right-click and select **Finish Freeform** in the marking menu.

Once closed, the ribbon updates and you can access the parametric modeling tools and the Model browser adds a **Form** feature to the list of features. To reactivate the Freeform environment, right-click on the **Form** feature node and select **Edit Freeform** (shown in Figure 4–11), or double-click on the **Form** node.

Figure 4–11

4.2 Editing Freeform Geometry

The *Freeform* tab provides editing tools (shown in Figure 4–12) that enable you to further refine the freeform geometry. As changes are made to the geometry they are all incorporated into the Form feature. Feature history is not recorded to account for each of the edits. While in the same session you can undo actions, but once the model has been saved the undo history is cleared.

Figure 4–12

The mesh that overlays the geometry is used for editing. The overall mesh consists of points that are connected by edges and the enclosed edges are called *faces*. While editing you can select points, edges, faces, loops, or bodies for editing. The Box freeform shown in Figure 4–13 identifies what each of the entity types refer to in the model.

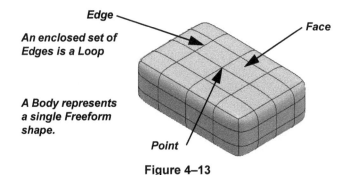

Figure 4–13

The following describes how you can use the available editing tools to manipulate the freeform shape.

Edit Form

The **Edit Form** command in the Freeform panel is the primary command that is used to manipulate geometry. It enables you to select point, edges, faces, bodies, or loops to access a manipulator triad that can be dragged to change the shape of the freeform.

How To: Edit Elements

1. In the *Freeform* tab>Edit panel, click  (Edit Form). The Edit Form dialog box opens, as shown in Figure 4–14.

Figure 4–14

2. In the *Filter* area, select the element type that is to be manipulated. The options include the following:

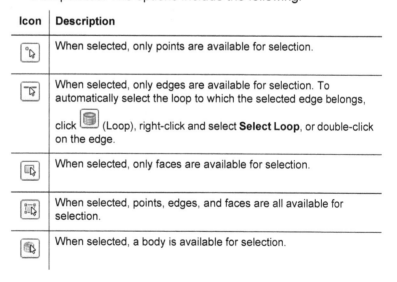

Icon	Description
	When selected, only points are available for selection.
	When selected, only edges are available for selection. To automatically select the loop to which the selected edge belongs, click (Loop), right-click and select **Select Loop**, or double-click on the edge.
	When selected, only faces are available for selection.
	When selected, points, edges, and faces are all available for selection.
	When selected, a body is available for selection.

To select multiple entities for simultaneous manipulation, hold <Shift> while selecting.

Once an element has been selected, a manipulator triad displays, as shown in Figure 4–15. The triad center is placed on the selected reference entity that is displayed in blue.

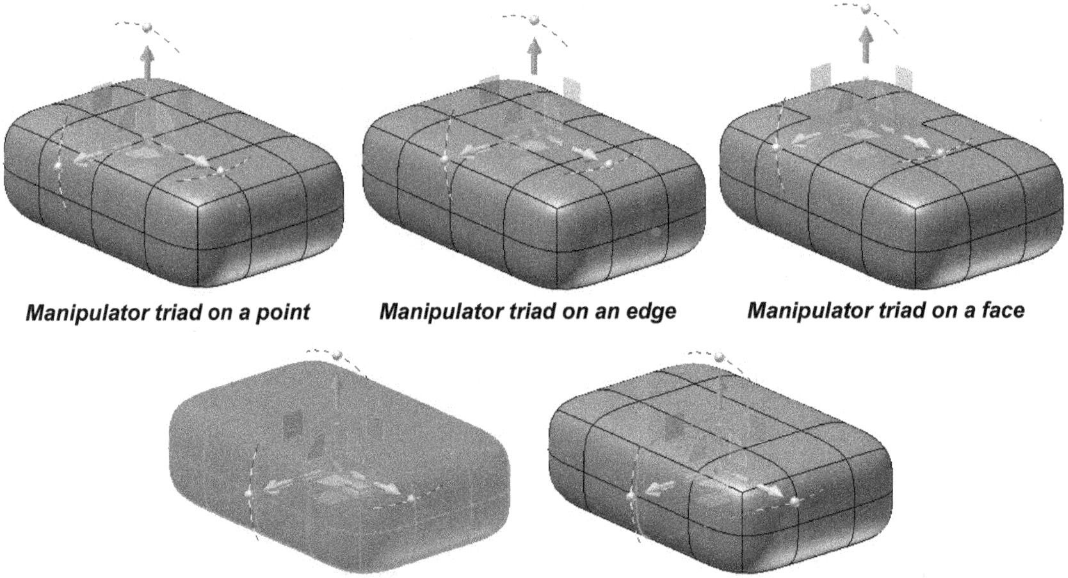

Manipulator triad on a point

Manipulator triad on an edge

Manipulator triad on a face

Manipulator triad on a body

Manipulator triad on a loop

Figure 4–15

3. (Optional) Filter the manipulator types that are displayed on the triad using the *Mode* settings in the *Transform* area. The available options enable you to determine whether it displays controls for ( ) Translation, (Rotation), (Scaling) or all of the controls at the same time ( ), as shown in Figure 4–16. The default setting is to show all of the manipulator types.

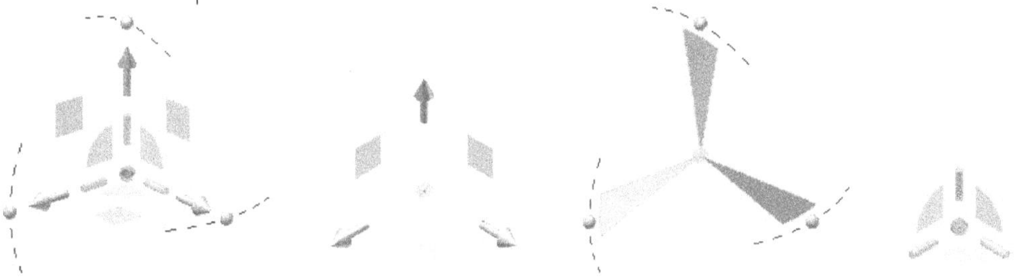

All types

Translation

Rotation

Scale

Figure 4–16

4. Define the *Space* setting in the *Transform* area. It enables you to control the orientation of the manipulator triad.

- Use (World) to set the orientation with the model origin orientation.

- Use (View) to set the orientation relative to the current view of the model.

- Use (Local) to set the orientation relative to the selected object.

*Alternatively, you can select **Locate** in the mini-toolbar to reset the triad's location.*

5. (Optional) Click (Locate) to reset the location of the manipulator triad on the geometry (not the element). Once active, select a new edge or point to locate the triad.
   - Faces cannot be selected as new references.

6. Select the remaining options as required:

- Click (Display) to toggle the model display from a smooth to blocky display style.

- Click (Extrude) in the *Transform* area to set the editing tool to entirely extrude a selected face instead of transforming it. If used, additional edges, faces, and points are created, as shown in Figure 4–17.

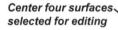

Center four surfaces selected for editing

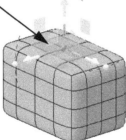  

Extrude Disabled   **Extrude Enabled**

Figure 4–17

***Soft Modification** is not available if the **Extrude** option is being used.*

- Click **Soft Modification** to enable the edit actions to have a more gradual impact on adjacent surfaces. When enabled, you are provided additional controls to define the *Type* and *Falloff* for the modification.

- Click (Reset) to clear all of the edits.

- Use (Undo) and (Redo) to clear or redo edits.

7. Reposition the geometry using either of the following:
    *   Select the controls directly on the triad to reposition the geometry. Each control on the triad enables you to manipulate the geometry in a different way. Figure 4–18 shows the controls and describes their uses. You can only manipulate one triad at a time.

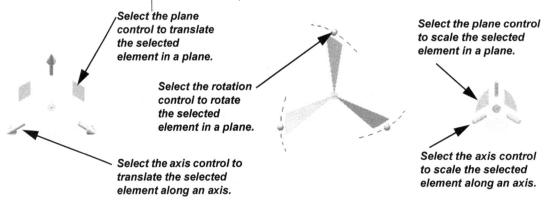

Select the plane control to translate the selected element in a plane.

Select the rotation control to rotate the selected element in a plane.

Select the axis control to translate the selected element along an axis.

Select the plane control to scale the selected element in a plane.

Select the axis control to scale the selected element along an axis.

Figure 4–18

*   Enter values in the mini-toolbar entry field. The available field depends on the active triad control. For example, if the y-axis is selected for translational movement,

    `Y: 0.0 ▶` is available in the mini-toolbar for entry. This value is not parametric and is not tied to the model.

8. Continue to select elements on the freeform model and make changes, as required.
9. Click **OK** to complete the edit.

Figure 4–19 shows the final geometry after multiple edits were made to a Box and Cylinder freeform shape.

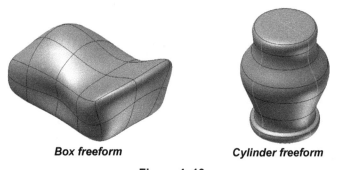

Box freeform   *Cylinder freeform*

Figure 4–19

Working with Edges

There are a number of different editing tools on the Modify panel that can be used to modify the edges of freeform geometry. These tools include the following:

- Insert Edge
- Merge Edges
- Unweld Edges
- Crease Edges
- Uncrease Edges
- Match Edge

Insert Edge

Additional edges can be added to a freeform using the **Insert Edge** command. By adding edges you can provide additional references (edges and the points at the end of edges) that can be modified to refine the shape of the model.

How To: Insert a New Edge(s)

1. In the *Freeform* tab>Modify panel, click ✧ (Insert Edge). The Insert Edge dialog box is shown in Figure 4–20.

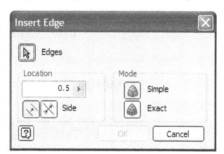

Figure 4–20

2. Click ⬚ (Edges) and select an existing edge in the model as a reference.
3. Enter an offset value in the *Location* area to define where the new edge is going to be located relative to the referenced edge. If the new edge is not created on the correct side, enter a negative value to switch sides.

4. Click ⬚ (Single) or ⬚ (Both) to create a new single edge at the defined location or to create edges on both sides of the reference, respectively.

5. Set the mode that should be used to define the final geometry once the edge is inserted.

- Click ⬤ (Simple mode) to add the new edge exactly as specified. The shape might change to add the edge.

- Click ⬤ (Exact mode), which while adding the new edge as specified, also adds any additional edges that might be required to enable the model to retain its current shape.

6. Click **OK** to insert the edge.

The images shown in Figure 4–21 show how two edges are inserted and how the overall shape changes when the edges are added.

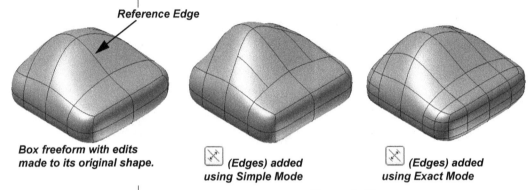

Reference Edge

Box freeform with edits made to its original shape.

⬤ *(Edges) added using Simple Mode*

⬤ *(Edges) added using Exact Mode*

Figure 4–21

Merge Edges

Use the **Merge Edges** command to merge two open freeform edges. This can be used to blend between two freeform bodies or two edges in a single body, if the geometry permits.

How To: Merge Edges

1. In the *Freeform* tab>Modify panel, click ✏ (Merge Edges). The Merge Edge dialog box is shown in Figure 4–22.

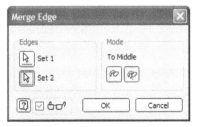

Figure 4–22

2. Click 🔲 (Set 1) and select an existing edge in the model as a reference.

3. Click 🔲 (Set 2), and select a second open edge to merge to. If the geometry can be created based on your selections, a preview of the geometry displays.

4. Set the **Mode** options to control the final geometry, as required.

   - Use 🔲 (To Edge) to blend to the second edge selection.

   - Use 🔲 (To Middle) to blend to the midpoint of the two edge selections.

5. Click **OK** to complete the merge.

Figure 4–23 shows how two edges are merged.

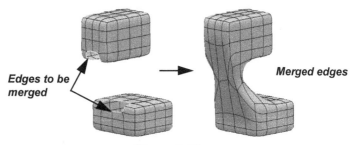

Edges to be merged

Merged edges

Figure 4–23

Unweld Edges

The 🔲 (Unweld Edges) option in the Modify panel enables you to select edges to separate them from the remaining freeform body. To unweld, simply select the edge or loop of edges and click **OK**. Once unwelded, multiple bodies are created that can be moved independently, as shown in Figure 4–24.

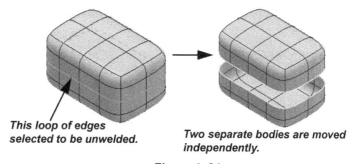

This loop of edges selected to be unwelded.

Two separate bodies are moved independently.

Figure 4–24

Crease/Uncrease Edges

The 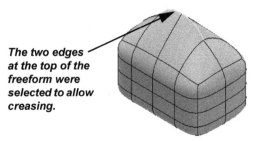 (Crease Edge) option in the Modify panel enables you to create non-curvature continuous edges on a freeform body by selecting and moving an edge. In Figure 4–25, the two edges were set to allow creasing. Once set, they display as gray. To crease an edge, simply select the edge or loop of edges and click **OK**.

The two edges at the top of the freeform were selected to allow creasing.

Figure 4–25

To clear the crease setting, click (Uncrease Edges) and select the edges to be cleared. The crease is immediately removed and the geometry updates.

Match Edge

When designing a freeform shape, there might be a design requirement that it must match an existing solid edge or a defined sketch. To match the edge of a freeform with a geometrically constrained edge or sketch, you can use the **Match Edge** command.

How To: Match an Existing Freeform Edge with a Geometrically Constrained Edge

1. Click 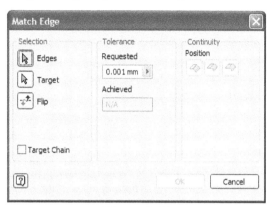 (Match Edge) in the Modify panel to open the Match Edge dialog box, shown in Figure 4–26.

Figure 4–26

2. Click (Edges) and select the freeform edge(s) that are to be modified to match the existing constrained geometry. If you are matching a fully enclosed entity, the freeform references must also be fully enclosed.

3. Click (Target) and select the existing edge/sketch in the model to match.

4. (Optional) Click (Flip), as required, to flip the direction of the match once the references are selected.

The Requested value must be less than the Achieved value for the match to be successful.

5. In the *Tolerance* area, enter the tolerance value to attempt to meet. The freeform shape attempts to create a match with this value. If it cannot, you are prompted with an Achieved value.

6. (Optional) If the match edge is a NURB surface edge, you have access to set continuity options to further define the shape. The options enable you to maintain GO, G1, or G2 continuity with the reference.

7. Click **OK** to match the edges.

The images in Figure 4–27 represent a cylinder freeform in which three of its edges were matched to three parametric sketches.

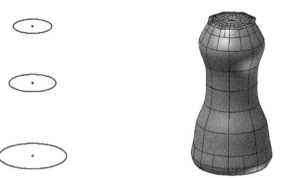

Three parametric sketches that define the top, middle, and bottom sizes of the model. **Match Edge used to match the edges at the top, middle, and bottom of the freeform with the parametric sketches.**

Figure 4–27

If the referenced edge that was used for matching changes, you can rematch the edge by expanding the *Matches* folder in the Form feature, right-clicking, and selecting **Rematch**, as shown in Figure 4–28.

Rematch can be used, when required to ensure that the match is maintained. This behavior does not happen automatically.

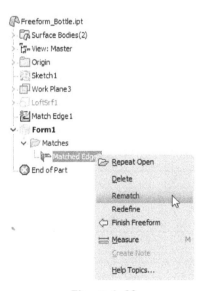

Figure 4–28

Working with Faces

The faces that make up a freeform mesh can also be manipulated to change the shape of freeform geometry. The **Subdivide** and **Bridge** commands enable you to manipulate a face.

Subdivide

The **Subdivide** command enables you to add additional faces to the model. The additional faces can help to refine the shape of the model.

How To: Subdivide an Existing Face

1. In the Modify panel, click (Subdivide) to open the Subdivide dialog box, shown in Figure 4–29.

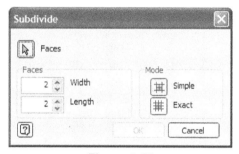

Figure 4–29

Hold <Shift> to select multiple faces for editing.

2. Click (Faces) and select an existing face in the model as a reference.
3. In the *Faces* area, enter values to define how the selected face is going to be subdivided.
4. Set the mode to be used to define the final geometry once the face is subdivided:

   • Click (Simple mode) to subdivide exactly as specified. The shape may change to add faces.

   • Click (Exact mode), which while adding the face as specified, also adds any additional faces that might be required to enable the model to retain its current shape.

5. Click **OK** to insert the face(s).

The images in Figure 4–30 show how nine faces were added (**3** in *Length* and **3** in *Width*) on a reference face using both the **Simple** and **Exact** mode options.

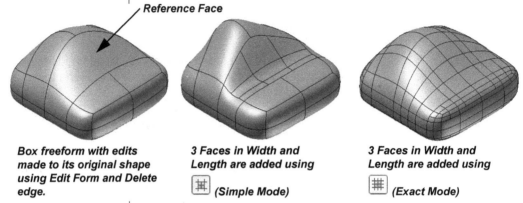

Reference Face

Box freeform with edits made to its original shape using Edit Form and Delete edge.

3 Faces in Width and Length are added using (Simple Mode)

3 Faces in Width and Length are added using (Exact Mode)

Figure 4–30

Bridge

When using multiple freeform bodies in a model, you can use the **Bridge** command to connect the space between the two shapes. Bridge can also be used to join multiple gaps in a single body.

How To: Create Bridge Geometry Between Existing Faces or Edges

1. Click (Bridge) in the Modify panel. The Bridge dialog box opens as shown in Figure 4–31.

Figure 4–31

Multiple faces can be selected for both the Side1 and Side2 references.

2. Click (Side1) and select existing faces or edges on the freeform model where the bridge geometry is going to begin.

3. Click (Side2) and select existing freeform faces or edges to which the bridge geometry is going to merge.

4. Enter a value in the *Faces* area to define the number of faces that the new bridge geometry is going to be subdivided into.
5. (Optional) Enter a value in the *Twists* area to define how many complete rotations there are going to be on the bridge geometry.
6. Click **OK** to create the bridge geometry.

The images in Figure 4–32 show how two separate cylindrical freeform shapes are bridged by new geometry and how it can be used in a single body to create a hole.

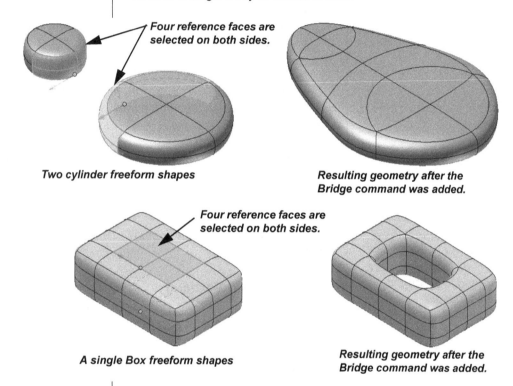

Four reference faces are selected on both sides.

Two cylinder freeform shapes

Resulting geometry after the Bridge command was added.

Four reference faces are selected on both sides.

A single Box freeform shapes

Resulting geometry after the Bridge command was added.

Figure 4–32

Working with Points

The points that define the edges and faces can also be modified using tools on the Modify panel. These tools include the following:

- Insert Point
- Weld Vertices
- Flatten

Insert Point

Similar to inserting edges, points can be inserted using a similar workflow. An edge is defined when multiple points are inserted, which also defines a new face.

How To: Insert Points

1. In the Modify panel, click ✦ (Insert Point).
   - By default, the **Insert Point** command is located in the **Insert Edge** drop-down list. Subsequently, the most recent command used is displayed.
2. Select points on edges to place new points.
3. Select the *Mode* to define the shape of the new points and subsequent edges. The **Simple** and **Exact** options are the same as for when inserting edges.
4. Click **OK**.

The new point breaks the edge and creates multiple edges to fully define any adjacent faces.

Weld Vertices

Consider using this option to combine vertices once edges are merged to refine the faces that are generated.

The **Weld Vertices** option enables you to combine two selected vertices.

How To: Weld Vertices

1. In the Modify panel, click ⬗ (Weld Vertices).
2. Select two points to weld.
3. Select one of the following **Weld Mode** options to customize the geometry that results from welding the vertices.

   - Select ⬚ (Vertex to Vertex) to merge two selected vertices. The first vertex is moved to the position of the second vertex.

   - Select ⬚ (Vertex to Midpoint) to move two selected vertices to the midpoint between the selections.

   - Select ⬚ (Weld to Tolerance) to combine multiple vertices within a specified tolerance. Select the vertices and then set the *Tolerance* value.
4. Click **OK** to weld the points.

Flatten

You must select more than 3 vertices to be able to flatten.

The **Flatten** option enables you to select multiple vertices and force them to flatten to a single plane.

How To: Flatten Points

1. In the Modify panel, click ⁙ (Flatten).
2. Select all the points to flatten.
3. In the *Direction* area, select an option to define how the points will flatten. The options include:

   • Use ⊞ (Auto Fit) to move points to a single plane that passes through the vertices.

   • Use ⊞ (Plane) to move points through a specified plane.

   • Use ⊞ (Parallel Plane) to move points parallel to a selected plane.

4. Click **OK** to flatten the selected points.

Figure 4–33 shows how the **Flatten** option was used to flatten multiple vertices so that they are parallel with a selected plane.

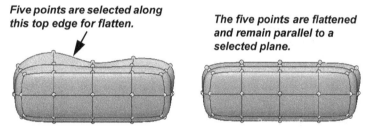

Five points are selected along this top edge for flatten.

The five points are flattened and remain parallel to a selected plane.

Figure 4–33

Thickening Freeform Geometry

The **Thicken** command can be used with freeform geometry to:

• Convert an open surface to a solid with soft or sharp edges.

• Create an offset surface.

• Create an interior or exterior wall if the selected freeform body is solid.

How To: Thicken a Freeform Body

1. In the Modify panel, click 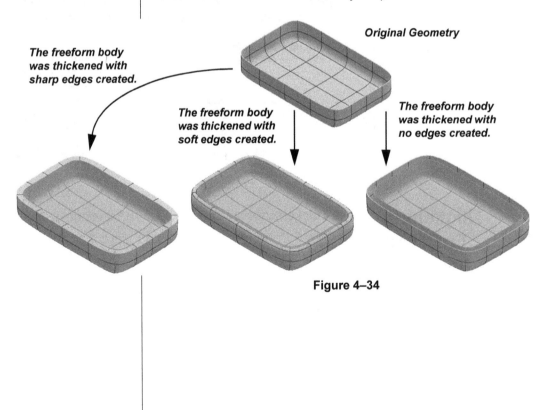 (Thicken)
2. In the *Type* area, select how the thickened geometry is capped. This is only available when thickening an open body. The possible options include:

   - Use ⬚ (Sharp) to create a flat face to bridge the offset.

   - Use ⬚ (Soft) to create a new face that is rounded to bridge the offset.

   - Use ⬚ (No Edges) to leave an open gap between the thickened geometry.

3. Enter a thickness value.
4. Select the direction of the offset. The options include normal to the selected body or in a selected direction. To define a direction, you must select an axis.
5. Click **OK** to thicken the selected body.

Figure 4–34 shows some examples of geometry that has been thickened when the selected body is open.

The freeform body was thickened with sharp edges created.

Original Geometry

The freeform body was thickened with soft edges created.

The freeform body was thickened with no edges created.

Figure 4–34

> **Hint: Reviewing Internal Geometry**
>
> When the **Thicken** command is used, geometry can be
> created internally. Click  (Toggle Translucent) to better
> visualize the internal geometry.

Controlling Symmetry

When the base freeform shape was created, symmetry could
have been defined for the overall geometry. The **Symmetry**
option enables you to define internal symmetry between selected
faces on the freeform body after the base feature creation.

How To: Apply Symmetry Between Faces

1. In the Symmetry panel, click ⬙ (Symmetry). The Symmetry
   dialog box is shown in Figure 4–35.

Figure 4–35

2. Click ⬚ (Face1) and select the face on side 1 as the
   reference for symmetry. The reference displays in blue on the
   model.

3. Click ⬚ (Face2) and select the face that is to be symmetric
   on the other side of the model. The reference displays in
   green on the model.

4. Click **OK** to assign symmetry.

*If symmetry cannot be
assigned based on the
references that are
selected you are
prompted to retry
making selections.*

The two images shown at the top of Figure 4–36 indicate how changes are made to the base freeform to which symmetry has not been assigned. The two images shown at the bottom indicate how two faces that have been assigned to be symmetric are updated when a change is made to one of the faces.

Box freeform shape - no symmetry set

Face edited using Edit Form.

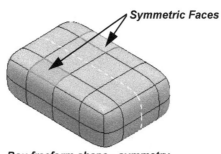

Symmetric Faces

Box freeform shape - symmetry assigned to two faces

Face edited using Edit Form (both symmetric faces update)

Figure 4–36

Symmetry assigned when the base freeform geometry was created cannot be cleared using this option.

- Symmetry that has been explicitly assigned between faces can be cleared by clicking (Clear Symmetry) in the expanded Symmetry drop-down list.

Mirroring Freeform Geometry

The (Mirror) command on the expanded Symmetry drop-down list enables you to mirror an entire freeform body about a selected plane.

How To: Complete the Mirror

1. In the Symmetry panel, click (Mirror).

2. Click (Body) and select the body that is to be mirrored. Only bodies can be selected for mirroring.

3. Click 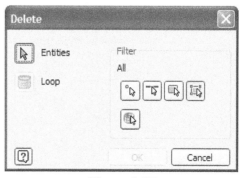 (Mirror Plane) and select a plane to mirror about.
4. If the mirrored body has an open edge and is to be merged with the original body, click **Weld** and enter a tolerance value. Based on the tolerance value, the two bodies will be merged, if possible.
5. Click **OK** to complete the mirror.

> **Hint: Repositioning a Freeform Body**
>
> When modeling or mirroring the location of the body relative to a required plane, the body's location may not be as required. To move the body, use either of the following commands:
>
> - Use the **Edit Form** command. Select the entire body and use the translation arrows to move it.
>
> - Use the **Align Form** command. With (Vertex) enabled select a vertex on the freeform body and then select a target plane to align to. If the geometry has defined symmetry, the (Symmetry Plane) option is used by default and you can align the symmetry plane to a target plane.

Deleting Entities

The mesh layout of a freeform shape may include too many points, edges, and faces. The **Delete** option enables you to delete points, edges, loops of edges, faces, and entire bodies. To open the Delete dialog box (shown in Figure 4–37), click (Delete) in the Edit panel.

Delete

    Entities   Filter

    Loop   All

Figure 4–37

To delete entities, simply select them and click **OK**. Consider using the options in the *Filter* area to control the type of entities allowed for selection. As an alternative, you can right-click on an entity and select **Delete**. A feature history is not recorded, so keep in mind that once the freeform is finished, edits can't be undone. Figure 4–38 shows how the **Delete** command is being used to delete points, edges, and faces on a freeform shape.

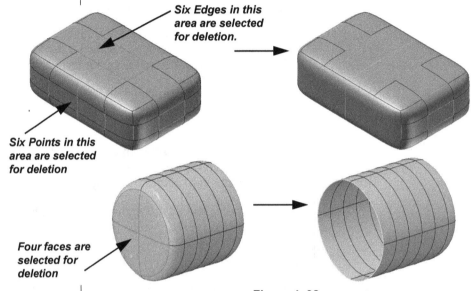

Figure 4–38

Hint: Selecting Faces

Toggle the 📐 (Select Through) option on the Tools panel to control how faces in a selection window are selected. When on, the selection includes hidden faces. When toggled off, the selection only includes the visible faces that fall in the selection window.

Practice 4a | Box Freeform Modeling

Practice Objectives

- Create freeform base geometry using the **Box** command.
- Toggle the view display from a smooth to block visual display style.
- Edit freeform base geometry so that points, edges, and faces are translated and rotated.
- Subdivide, delete, and insert elements on freeform base geometry to permit changes to the shape of the geometry.

In this practice, you will learn how create a box-shaped freeform model and to navigate the Freeform modeling environment. Using the Edit Form and additional editing tools you will manipulate the shape of the box.

Task 1 - Create a Box freeform shape.

1. Create a new part with the default mm template.

2. In the *3D Model* tab>Create Freeform panel, click 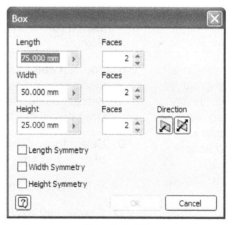 (Box). The Box dialog box opens (as shown in Figure 4–39), providing options that enable you to define the shape of the Box freeform geometry.

Figure 4–39

3. The Origin planes are temporarily displayed in the graphics window (as shown in Figure 4–40), so that you can select the sketch plane.

Figure 4–40

4. Hover the cursor over the origin planes in the graphics window. Note that the names display directly on the work planes in the graphics window.

5. Locate and select the XY Plane as the sketch plane.

6. Use the ViewCube to return the model to its default orientation.

7. By default, the Origin Center Point is projected onto the XY sketch plane. Select the center point as the base point for the Box.

*To display the Origin 3D Indicator in the graphics window to help identify directions, open the Application Options dialog box and enable **Show Origin 3D Indicator** on the Display tab.*

8. You can enter values for the *Length*, *Width*, and *Height* or select manipulator arrowheads on the geometry. Select the x-direction arrowhead (*Length*) and drag it to enlarge the box. Drag it until the box is approximately **100mm**.

9. Select the y-direction arrowhead (*Width*) and drag it to a size of approximately **60mm**.

10. In the Box dialog box, set the *Height* value to **25**.

11. Ensure that exact values are entered for *Length*, *Width*, and *Height*, as shown in Figure 4–41.

12. Ensure that ⬚ (Direction) is selected to create the freeform above the XY plane.

13. Select **Width Symmetry** to maintain symmetry on both sides of the XZ plane.

14. To define the number of faces on each plane of the model, enter the *Face* values in the Box dialog box, as shown in Figure 4–41. Once all of the settings have been set, the model updates as shown on the right.

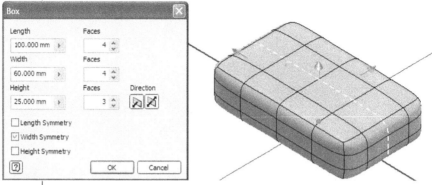

Figure 4–41

15. Click **OK** to complete the Box. The *Freeform* tab is activated.

16. In the *Freeform* tab>Tools panel, click 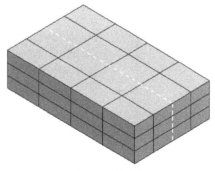 (Toggle Smooth). The model switches from a smooth display to a block display style, as shown in Figure 4–42. This is a display type only, which can increase performance speed. The model is still smooth when it is toggled off or when Freeform mode is off.

Figure 4–42

17. Click 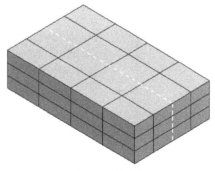 (Toggle Smooth) again to return to the smooth display style.

Task 2 - Edit the Freeform geometry.

1. In the Edit panel, click  (Edit Form). The Edit Form dialog box opens as shown in Figure 4–43.

Figure 4–43

2. Note that in the *Filter* area, (All) is set as the default option. If it is not selected, do so. This enables you to select any point, edge, or face on the model. Hover the cursor over the points, edges, and faces in the model. Note that you can select any of them. Selecting the other options filters the selection to points only, edges only, or faces only, which can be useful when working with complex freeform geometry with large mesh structures.

3. Select the vertex shown in Figure 4–44 to be translated.

4. Select the z-axis manipulator arrowhead (as shown in Figure 4–44) and drag upwards similar to that shown.

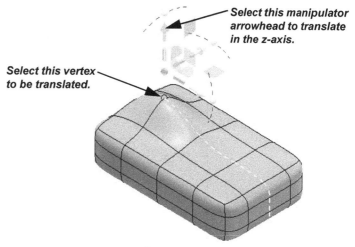

Select this manipulator arrowhead to translate in the z-axis.

Select this vertex to be translated.

Figure 4–44

5. Select the face shown in Figure 4–45 to be translated.

6. Select the z-axis manipulator arrowhead (as shown in Figure 4–45), and drag upwards similar to that shown. Note that both sides update together. This is because the **Width Symmetry** option was used when the box was created.

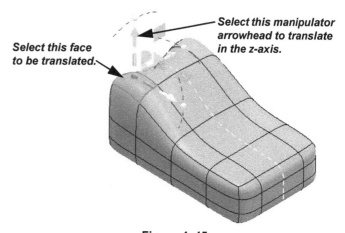

Select this manipulator arrowhead to translate in the z-axis.

Select this face to be translated.

Figure 4–45

7. Select the face shown in Figure 4–46 to be translated.

8. Select the manipulator wheel shown in Figure 4–46, and drag upwards to rotate the face in the XZ plane. Note that both sides update together.

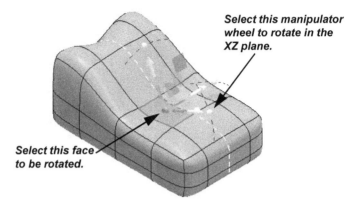

Select this manipulator wheel to rotate in the XZ plane.

Select this face to be rotated.

Figure 4–46

9. Select the front edge shown in Figure 4–47 to be translated.

10. Select the x-axis manipulator shown in Figure 4–47, and drag outward in the x-axis. Both sides update together.

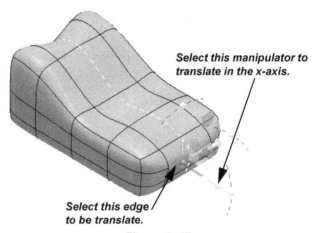

Select this manipulator to translate in the x-axis.

Select this edge to be translate.

Figure 4–47

11. In the Edit Form dialog box, click ⟲ to undo the last change to the model.

12. Select the same edge again, if not still selected and click

    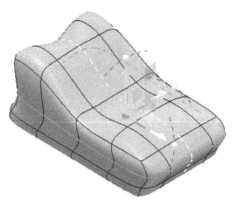 is not at this position

    (Loop) in the *Selection Options* area of the Edit Form dialog box. Alternatively, right-click and select **Select Loop**. The loop in which the edge exists highlights. Drag the same manipulator handle. The model displays similar to that shown in Figure 4–48. The entire loop of edges translate forward.

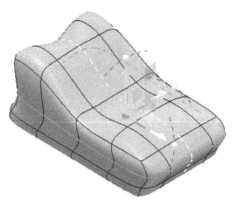

Figure 4–48

13. Click ✓ to complete the edit.

In Freeform mode all of the parametric model commands are not available.

14. Save the file as **Freeform_Box.ipt**. Note that the model cannot be saved in Freeform mode. Click **Cancel**.

15. In the *Freeform* tab>Exit panel, click ✓ (Finish Freeform). Alternatively, right-click in the graphics window and select **Finish Freeform** in the marking menu. Note that the model displays as solid geometry, as shown in Figure 4–49.

The default visual display for new models is Shaded with Edges. To clear the display of the edges, you can change to the Shaded display style.

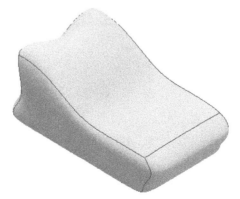

Figure 4–49

16. Save the file as **Freeform_Box.ipt**.

Task 3 - Use Edit tools to further customize the meshed structure of the freeform.

1. In the *3D Model* tab, note that all of the parametric model commands are now available. You can continue to design the model using the familiar parametric commands. To further edit the freeform geometry, right-click on the **Form1** feature in the Model browser and select **Edit Freeform**.

2. The middle portion needs to be subdivided to include more faces. In the Modify panel, click ☜ (Subdivide) to open the Subdivide dialog box.

3. Click 🖮 (Faces) if it is not already active, and select the face shown in Figure 4–50. Note that the symmetry setting that was assigned during Box creation still persists.

4. Accept the default value for the number of faces in the *Width* and *Length* fields, as shown in Figure 4–50.

5. For the *Mode* setting, maintain 🖽 (Simple).

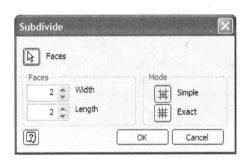
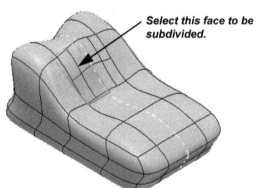

Select this face to be subdivided.

Figure 4–50

6. Click **OK** to insert the face(s). Note that the geometry changed slightly to permit the subdivision. This was acceptable. If the change is not, click 🖽 (Exact) in the Subdivide dialog box when creating it. The geometry shape will stay the same but additional faces are added to maintain the shape.

7. In the Freeform panel, click ☜ (Edit Form).

8. Select one of the edges generated by the subdivide action, (as shown in Figure 4–51) and click 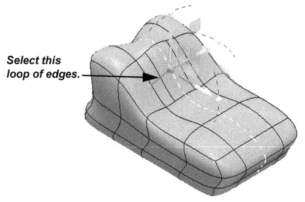 (Loop) or right-click and select **Select Loop** to automatically select all of the adjacent edges.

Select this loop of edges.

Figure 4–51

9. In the Edit Form dialog box, in the *Transform* area, click  (View). The triad changes to only display two axis manipulators, as shown in Figure 4–52.

Figure 4–52

10. In the ViewCube, select the **Right** view. Note that the triad updates to display the Manipulators in the new orientation, while retaining the x- and y-directions for the view.

11. Right-click in the graphics window and select **Previous View**. The edge remains selected. If it does not, select the loop again.

12. In the *Transform* area, click 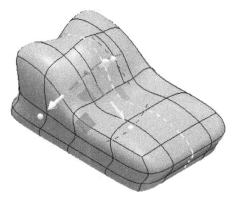 (Local) to change the triad location to the Local orientation. Drag the manipulators to create the geometry shown in Figure 4–53.

Figure 4–53

13. Click **OK** to complete the edit.

Task 4 - Delete edges from the freeform geometry.

---

1. Now that the reshaping is done you can delete edges in the area that was subdivided. In the Edit panel, click (Delete).

2. In the Delete dialog box, click 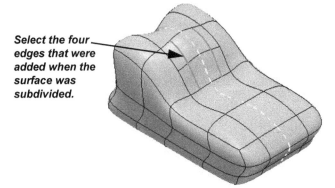 (Edge) and select the four edges shown in Figure 4–54.

Select the four edges that were added when the surface was subdivided.

Figure 4–54

3. Click **OK** to delete the edges. The model updates as shown in Figure 4–55. Alternatively, because the Box was created symmetrically in the width direction, selecting two edges on one side would also have deleted the edges on the other side.

Figure 4–55

Task 5 - Insert edges on freeform geometry.

1. In the Modify panel, click 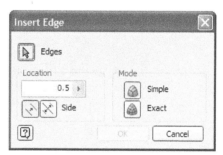 (Insert Edge). The Insert Edge dialog box opens as shown in Figure 4–56.

Figure 4–56

2. Click ⬚ (Edges) if it is not already active, and select the edge shown in Figure 4–57. A preview of the new edge displays immediately.

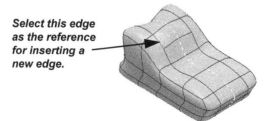

Select this edge as the reference for inserting a new edge.

Figure 4–57

3. In the *Location* area, set the offset value to **0.2**. The edge moves closer to the reference edge.

4. Return the value to **0.5** to create the new edge midway between the reference edge the next edge.

5. In the *Mode* area, click  (Exact). If Simple mode had been used the geometry would change to create the edge. In this situation the exact shape must be retained so Exact mode is used.

6. Click **OK** to insert the edit. The new edge is created, but to keep both symmetry and the existing shape, more edges have been added, as shown in Figure 4–58.

Figure 4–58

7. In the *Freeform* tab>Exit panel, click ✔ (Finish Freeform). Alternatively, right-click in the graphics window and select **Finish Freeform** in the marking menu.

8. Save the file and close the window.

Practice 4b

Cylinder Freeform Modeling

Practice Objectives

- Create freeform base geometry using the **Cylinder** command.
- Match edges on the freeform base geometry to that of parametric sketch geometry.
- Assign symmetry to faces on the freeform base geometry.
- Cancel assigned symmetry between faces on the freeform base geometry.
- Use the **Edit Form** command to scale elements on the freeform base geometry.

In this practice, you will learn how to create a Cylinder as the freeform base geometry. You will also assign symmetry so that when editing faces on the cylinder, the change is also mirrored on the model. Additionally, you will use the **Match Edge** command to assign an edge on the freeform model equal to that of a parametric sketch.

Task 1 - Create a sketch that will be referenced by a freeform cylinder.

1. Create a new part using the default mm template.

2. In the *3D Model* tab>Sketch panel, click ⬚ (Start 2D Sketch).

3. Select the XY Plane as the sketch plane.

4. Create a circle with a diameter of **70mm** centered on the projected Origin Center Point.

5. Complete the sketch.

6. Toggle off the dimension visibility for the sketch.

Task 2 - Create a freeform cylinder.

1. In the *3D Model* tab>Create Freeform panel, click

    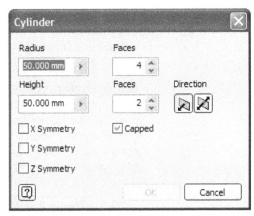 (Cylinder). The Cylinder dialog box (shown in Figure 4–59) opens providing options for defining the shape of the Cylinder freeform geometry.

Figure 4–59

2. Locate and select the XY Plane as the sketch plane.

3. Select the projected Origin Center Point as the base point for the Cylinder.

4. In the Cylinder dialog box, click ▧ to ensure that the freeform geometry is centered on both sides of the sketch plane.

5. You can enter values for the *Radius* and *Height* or select the manipulator arrowheads on the geometry. Using either technique, create the cylinder so that its *Radius* is **40** and its *Height* is **200**.

Symmetry assigned during freeform creation always remains with the geometry. Adding symmetry using the editing tools provides the flexibility to add and remove it, as required.

6. Symmetry will be assigned using the **Symmetry** command in the editing tools. Ensure that symmetry is not specified in the Cylinder dialog box.

7. To define the number of faces on each plane of the model, enter the *Face* values shown on the left in Figure 4–60.

8. Ensure that **Capped** is selected. Once all of the settings have been set, the model updates as shown on the right in Figure 4–60.

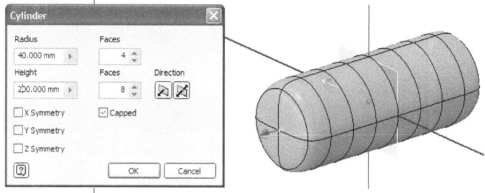

Figure 4–60

9. Click **OK** to complete the Cylinder.

Task 3 - Match an edge on the freeform geometry with the sketch.

---

1. In the Modify panel click 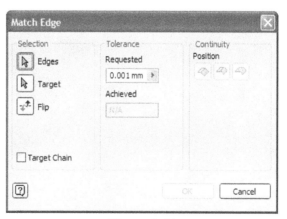 (Match Edge). The Match dialog box opens as shown in Figure 4–61.

Figure 4–61

If you are matching a fully enclosed entity, the freeform references must also be a fully enclosed loop.

2. Click 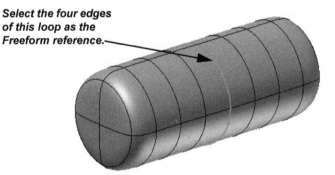 (Edges) if it is not already active, and select the freeform edges shown in Figure 4–62 to match the circular sketch.

Select the four edges of this loop as the Freeform reference.

Figure 4–62

3. Click (Target) and select the existing circular sketch as the Match reference.

4. Maintain the default tolerance value.

5. Click **OK** to match the edges. The freeform geometry updates as shown in Figure 4–63.

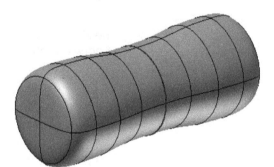

Figure 4–63

Task 4 - Assign Symmetry to the freeform geometry and edit the symmetric faces.

1. Return the model to its default orientation using the ViewCube.

2. In the Edit panel, click 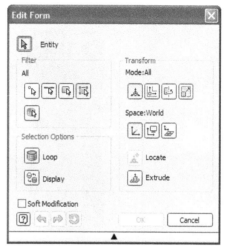 (Edit Form). The Edit Form dialog box opens as shown in Figure 4–64.

Figure 4–64

3. In the *Filter* area, ensure that either 🔲 (All) or 🔲 (Face) is selected and select the face shown in Figure 4–65 to be translated.

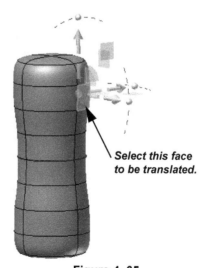

Select this face to be translated.

Figure 4–65

4. In the Edit Form dialog box, in the *Transform* area, click
   (View). The triad changes to only display two axis
   manipulators.

5. In the ViewCube, select the edge between the Right and
   Bottom sides, as shown in Figure 4–66.

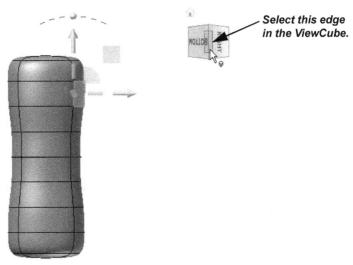

Figure 4–66

6. Select the x-axis manipulator arrowhead and drag it to the
   right, similar to that shown in Figure 4–67.

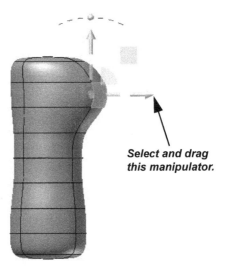

Figure 4–67

7. In the Edit Form dialog box, click  (Reset) to reset any of the changes made in the command. Click **Yes** to confirm the reset.

8. Click **Cancel** to close the Edit Form dialog box.

9. In the Symmetry panel, click ◢ (Symmetry). The Symmetry dialog box is shown in Figure 4–68.

Figure 4–68

10. Click ⬚ (Face1) if it is not already active, and select the face shown in Figure 4–69. The reference displays in blue.

11. Click ⬚ (Face2) and select the face shown in Figure 4–69 as the symmetric reference on the other side of the model. The reference displays in green on the model.

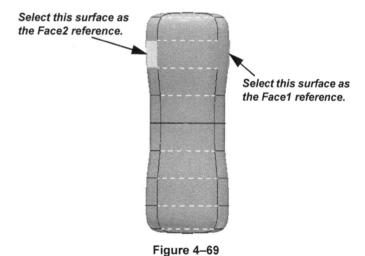

Figure 4–69

12. Click **OK** to assign the symmetry.

13. Use the **Edit Form** command again to translate the face that was just translated in the x-axis direction. Now that symmetry has been assigned with this surface, its symmetric face is also selected. Ensure that 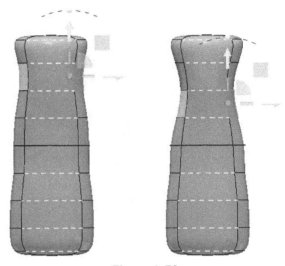 (View Space) is set and that the ViewCube is oriented as was previously set.

14. Drag the x-axis manipulator to translate the face inward, as shown on the left in Figure 4–70. Both symmetric faces update.

15. Select the surface below it and translate it inwards, as shown on the right in Figure 4–70. Note that it also reacts as symmetric.

Figure 4–70

16. Complete the edit.

17. In the Symmetry panel, expand the Symmetry drop-down list, and click (Clear Symmetry). Select the cylindrical body to clear its symmetry. Selecting this option clears all of the assigned symmetry. Symmetry assigned during freeform creation is not cleared with this option.

Task 5 - Ensure that the matched edges in the freeform remain matched.

1. Rotate the model to its default home view, as shown on the left in Figure 4–71. Note that the edge that was matched is no longer matched. The edits that were made have moved it. Matching does not maintain the relationship.

2. In the Model browser, expand **Form1** and the *Matches* folder. Right-click on **Matched Edge 1** and select **Rematch**. The matches edges are shown in Figure 4–71.

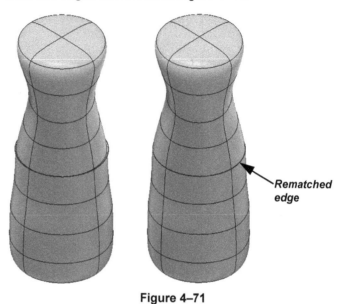

Rematched edge

Figure 4–71

Task 6 - Scale a face in the freeform geometry.

1. Start the **Edit Form** command.

2. In the *Transform* area, click 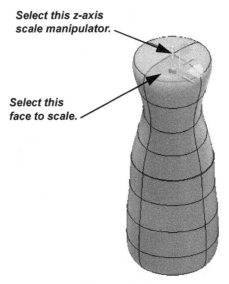 (Scale) to only display the scaling triad.

3. Select the face and scale manipulator in the z-axis as shown in Figure 4–72, and drag upward to scale the face.

Select this z-axis scale manipulator.

Select this face to scale.

Figure 4–72

4. Complete the edit.

5. Use the ViewCube to orient the model to the **Bottom** view and note that the scaling has changed the geometry on the face that was selected.

6. Right-click in the graphics window and select **Previous View**.

7. In the *Freeform* tab>Exit panel, click ✓ (Finish Freeform). Alternatively, right-click in the graphics window and select **Finish Freeform** in the marking menu.

8. Save the file as **Freeform_Cylinder.ipt** and close the window.

Practice 4c | Bridging Freeform Geometry

Practice Objective

- Create two freeform base geometry forms and use the **Bridge** command to generate additional geometry between the forms.

In this practice, you will create two cylinder freeform base shapes in the model to help when creating the required freeform geometry. Once created you will use the **Bridge** command to create additional geometry between the two cylinders.

Task 1 - Create a freeform cylinder.

1. Create a new part using the default mm template.

2. Use the Cylinder freeform feature to create the freeform, similar to that shown in Figure 4–73. Locate the cylinder on the XY Plane and use the projected Origin Center Point as the base point for the Cylinder.

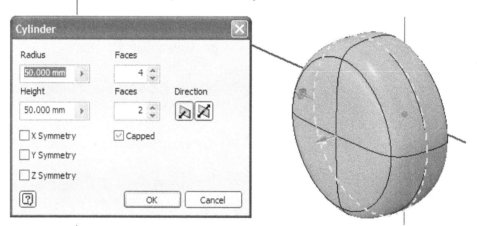

Figure 4–73

3. In the *Freeform* tab>Create Freeform panel, use the Cylinder freeform feature to create a second freeform, similar to that shown in Figure 4–74. Select the same plane, but use an origin point that is offset from the initial cylinder.

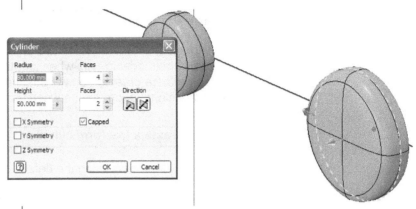

Figure 4–74

Task 2 - Create geometry between the two cylinders.

---

1. In the Modify panel, click 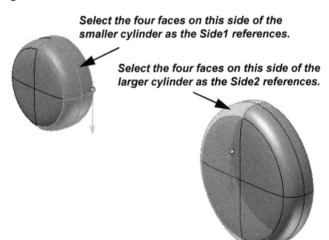 (Bridge).

2. Click ⬚ (Side1), if it is not already active, and select the four faces shown in Figure 4–75.

3. Click ⬚ (Side2) and select the four faces shown in Figure 4–75.

Select the four faces on this side of the smaller cylinder as the Side1 references.

Select the four faces on this side of the larger cylinder as the Side2 references.

Figure 4–75

4. Maintain the default faces for the number of faces and the twist.

5. Click **OK** to create the bridge geometry. The geometry displays as shown in Figure 4–76. Additional **Edit Form** actions can be performed on the new freeform feature, as required.

Figure 4–76

6. Exit the Freeform environment.

7. Save the file as **Freeform_Bridge.ipt** and close the window.

Chapter Review Questions

1. When modeling in the Freeform environment you can create parametric sketches for use with the **Match Edge** command.

   a. True

   b. False

2. Which of the following standard freeform shapes enables you to assign symmetry in the width, length, and height when creating the freeform base shape?

   a. Box

   b. Cylinder

   c. Sphere

   d. Torus

   e. Quadball

   f. Plane

3. The Quadball standard freeform shape enables you to assign faces along the longitude and latitude of the resulting shape.

   a. True

   b. False

4. Which of the following statements is true regarding symmetry in freeform geometry?

   a. Symmetry can only be assigned when the base freeform shape is created.

   b. Symmetry can only be assigned using the **Symmetry** command by selecting faces on the freeform geometry.

   c. All of the symmetry assigned on the base freeform shape can be removed using the **Clear Symmetry** command.

   d. Faces adjacent to a face that was selected as a symmetry reference also update to reflect the symmetry.

5. When using the **Edit Form** command, which of the following describe the manipulator controls that are available when the triad displays as shown in Figure 4–77? (Select all that apply.)

Figure 4–77

a. Translate in X, Y, or Z axis

b. Translate in plane

c. Rotate in plane

d. Scale in X, Y, or Z axis

e. Scale in plane

6. Which of the Space settings provides you with two manipulators that can be used to manipulate the freeform geometry?

a. (World)

b. (View)

c. (Local)

7. Which of the following editing commands enables you to add additional elements (points, edges, or faces) to existing freeform geometry? (Select all that apply.)

a. **Insert Edge**

b. **Insert Point**

c. **Subdivide**

d. **Crease Edges**

e. **Bridge**

f. **Match Edge**

8. The **Flatten** command enables you to select multiple points and make them parallel to a selected plane.

   a. True

   b. False

9. When subdividing a face, ⊞ (Simple mode) forces the freeform geometry to remain exactly the same once the faces have been subdivided.

   a. True

   b. False

10. Which of the following commands can be used to create the geometry between two freeform shapes? (Select all that apply.)

   a. **Insert Edge**

   b. **Subdivide**

   c. **Merge Edges**

   d. **Bridge**

   e. **Match Edge**

Answers: 1.b, 2.a, 3.b, 4.d, 5.(a,b), 6.b, 7.(a,b,c), 8.a, 9.b, 10.(c,d)

Command Summary

Button	Command	Location
	Align Form	• **Ribbon:** *Freeform* tab>Edit panel
	Box	• **Ribbon:** *3D Model* tab>Create Freeform panel • **Ribbon:** *Freeform* tab> Create Freeform panel
	Bridge	• **Ribbon:** *Freeform* tab> Modify panel
	Clear Symmetry	• **Ribbon:** *Freeform* tab>Symmetry panel
	Convert	• **Ribbon:** *3D Model* tab>Create Freeform panel • **Ribbon:** *Freeform* tab> Create Freeform panel
	Crease Edges	• **Ribbon:** *Freeform* tab>Modify panel
	Cylinder	• **Ribbon:** *3D Model* tab>Create Freeform panel • **Ribbon:** *Freeform* tab> Create Freeform panel
	Delete	• **Ribbon:** *Freeform* tab>Edit panel
	Edit Form	• **Ribbon:** *Freeform* tab>Edit panel
	Face	• **Ribbon:** *3D Model* tab>Create Freeform panel • **Ribbon:** *Freeform* tab> Create Freeform panel
	Finish Freeform	• **Ribbon:** *Freeform* tab> Exit panel • **Context menu:** In the graphics window
	Flatten	• **Ribbon:** *Freeform* tab> Modify panel
	Insert Edge	• **Ribbon:** *Freeform* tab>Modify panel
	Insert Point	• **Ribbon:** *Freeform* tab>Modify panel
	Match Edge	• **Ribbon:** *Freeform* tab>Modify panel
	Merge Edges	• **Ribbon:** *Freeform* tab>Modify panel
	Mirror	• **Ribbon:** *Freeform* tab>Symmetry panel

	Plane	• **Ribbon:** *3D Model* tab> Create Freeform panel
		• **Ribbon:** *Freeform* tab> Create Freeform panel
	Quadball	• **Ribbon:** *3D Model* tab>Create Freeform panel
		• **Ribbon:** *Freeform* tab> Create Freeform panel
	Select Through	• **Ribbon:** *Freeform* tab>Tools panel
	Sphere	• **Ribbon:** *3D Model* tab>Create Freeform panel
		• **Ribbon:** *Freeform* tab> Create Freeform panel
	Subdivide	• **Ribbon:** *Freeform* tab>Modify panel
	Symmetry	• **Ribbon:** *Freeform* tab>Symmetry panel
	Thicken	• **Ribbon:** *Freeform* tab> Modify panel
	Toggle Smooth/ Blocky	• **Ribbon:** *Freeform* tab>Tools panel
	Toggle Translucent	• **Ribbon:** *Freeform* tab> Tools panel
	Torus	• **Ribbon:** *3D Model* tab>Create Freeform panel
		• **Ribbon:** *Freeform* tab> Create Freeform panel
	Uncrease Edges	• **Ribbon:** *Freeform* tab>Modify panel
	Unweld Edges	• **Ribbon:** *Freeform* tab>Modify panel
	Weld Vertices	• **Ribbon:** *Freeform* tab>Modify panel

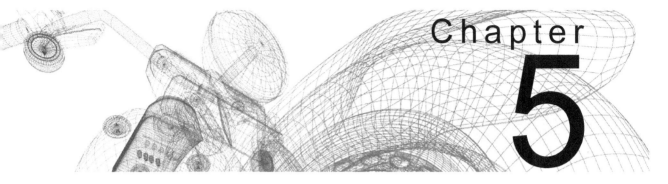

Chapter 5

Analyzing a Model

The ability to analyze models prior to manufacturing is a valuable tool in digital prototyping. The Autodesk® Inventor® software offers a variety of basic tools that can be used to verify such things as continuity, draft, curvature, and cross-sections in model geometry. Understanding how to use these tools during the design process helps to ensure that there are fewer issues prior to finalizing a model or sending it to a more complex analysis software tool.

Learning Objectives in this Chapter

- Conduct a Zebra analysis that evaluates continuity between surfaces.
- Conduct a Draft analysis that enables you to visually evaluate whether the applied draft values in a model are within a specified range.
- Conduct a Curvature analysis that evaluates whether continuity exists between surfaces based on the results of flow lines.
- Conduct a Gaussian, Mean Curvature, or Maximum Curvature analysis for points on a surface.
- Conduct a Cross Section analysis that displays the model sectioned through a single plane.
- Conduct a Cross Section analysis that displays the model sectioned through a series of planes and also identifies areas of the model that conflict with specified maximum and minimum wall thickness values.

5.1 Analysis Types

There are five analysis types that are available to analyze model geometry. These types are Zebra, Draft, Curvature, Surface, and Section.

Zebra Analysis

A Zebra Analysis projects parallel lines onto a model to determine if continuity between surfaces exists.

- If the stripes are parallel, the surface/face is flat.

- If the stripe edges do not line up, then the two surfaces are not tangent.

- If the stripe edges line up, but display a sharp angle, then the boundary is tangent but not curvature continuous.

- If the stripe edges are continuous (no sharp angles) across the boundary of two surfaces, then the transition is curvature continuous.

Figure 5–1 shows the three continuity options.

Stripe edges do not line up between surfaces (i.e., not tangent)

Stripe edges line up between surfaces; however there is a sharp angle (not continuous)

Stripe edges line up between surfaces and there is no sharp angle

Figure 5–1

Draft Analysis

A Draft Analysis determines if the drafts that have been added to the model are satisfactory for manufacturing. Based on a draft's maximum and minimum permissible values, a color gradient is displayed so that you can compare it to the model.

- If the draft falls within the permissible range (i.e., faces with adequate draft angles), the color of the selected faces/ surfaces can be distinguished in the color gradient.

- If the colors on the model are outside the gradient, the draft angle is outside the range and further analysis of the surface should be done.

Figure 5–2 shows an example of a model whose draft angle is within the permissible range.

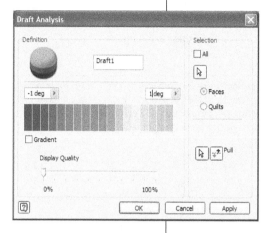

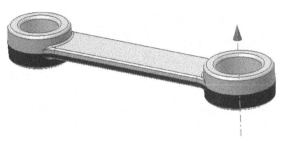

Figure 5–2

Curvature Analysis

An edge is generated where two surfaces meet, and a vertex is generated where two curves meet. The term continuity refers to how the faces/surfaces or end points meet. A Curvature analysis enables you to visually analyze the results of continuity calculations for flow lines (curvature comb) on selected faces or quilts or between them. The connections between curves and surfaces are described as follows:

G-1	Curves or surfaces <u>do not</u> share a common end point. There is no continuity.
G0	Curves or surfaces <u>do</u> share a common end point. They are not tangent to one another.

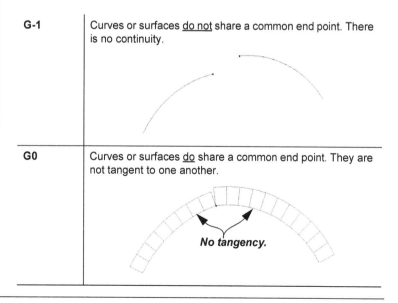

G1	Curves or surfaces are tangent to each other and share a common boundary, but have differing curvature magnitudes at their intersection.
	Entities are tangent.

G2	Curves or surfaces are tangent to each other and have a common curvature at their shared boundary. G2 continuity produces a smooth connection. G2 continuity is usually only required for surfaces in which light reflection is an issue.
	Tangent and curvature continuous.

Surface Analysis

Surface analysis tools provide three analysis types: Gaussian, Mean Curvature, and Maximum Curvature, as shown in Figure 5–3.

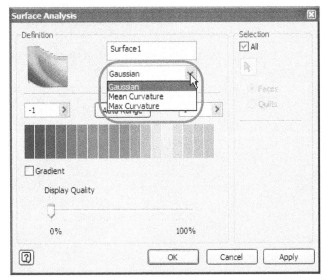

Figure 5–3

The three surface analysis types are described as follows:

- A **Gaussian** analysis is the product of the minimum curvature and maximum curvature for a given point on a surface. It is used to locate areas of high and low surface curvature and values can be either positive or negative. Minimum curvature values display in blue and maximum values display in green. All other values are assigned a color between blue and green. The Gaussian curvature for planar and cylindrical surfaces are zero because the curvature is always zero in at least one direction. Figure 5–4 shows a Gaussian Curvature analysis performed on two different parts.

Figure 5–4

- The **Mean Curvature** surface analysis provides information on the curvature of the u and v surfaces. Similar to a Gaussian analysis, it displays the results using a color gradient.

- The **Maximum Curvature** surface analysis shows the largest normal curvature at every point on the surface. Similar to a Gaussian analysis, it displays the results using a color gradient.

Cross Section Analysis

A Cross Section (Section) analysis obtains information about a cross-section through a part. You can perform two types of analyses: Simple and Advanced.

- A simple section analysis displays the model as a cutaway view of the part based on the selected plane and enables visual inspection. This view is similar to the slice graphics option, as shown in Figure 5–5.

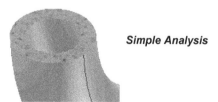

Simple Analysis

Figure 5–5

- An advanced section analysis enables you to define multiple
  section planes by either selecting or creating them. It can
  also verify the maximum and minimum wall thickness and
  area. For an advanced section analysis, areas in a section
  that are thicker than the maximum highlight in red on the
  model and are listed in the *Results* area. Areas thinner than
  the minimum part thickness highlight in blue on the model
  and are listed in the *Results* area. A sample Advanced
  Section analysis is shown in Figure 5–6, where the part
  contains one cross-section that is too thick, one that is within
  the thickness range, and one that is too thin.

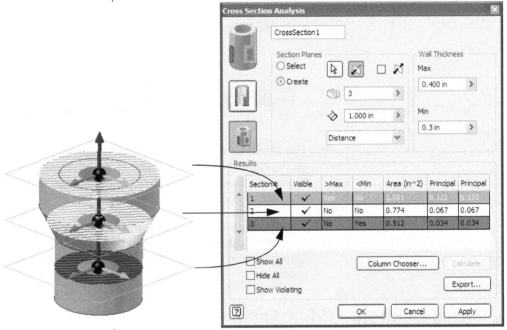

Figure 5–6

5.2 Analysis Procedures

Regardless of which analysis tool you use, the procedure for analyzing a model is similar.

General Steps

Use the following general steps to perform an analyses on a model:

1. Start the analysis.
2. Select the references.
3. Define the options.
4. Complete and review the analysis.
5. Display or edit an existing analysis.

Step 1 - Start the analysis.

In the *Inspect* tab>Analysis panel, select the required analysis type, as shown in Figure 5–7.

Figure 5–7

The corresponding dialog box opens. For all analyses, specify a name for the analysis or use the default.

- For a Surface Analysis, you must also select the type of surface analysis: **Gaussian**, **Mean Curvature**, or **Max Curvature**.

- For a Section Analysis you must also select the type of section analysis as **Simple** or **Advanced**.

Step 2 - Select the references.

Reference selection is required to define which geometry on the model is to be analyzed.

- For the Zebra, Draft, Curvature, and Surface analyses you must select surfaces to analyze. The default is to analyze all surfaces; however, you can clear the **All** option and select either **Faces** or **Quilts**, as shown in Figure 5–8. If either **Faces** or **Quilts** are to be used you must select the entities to analyze. For a Draft analysis, you must also select a reference for the pull direction.

Figure 5–8

- For a Section analyses, select a plane that cuts through the part at the required angle.

  - For a Simple Section analysis, an offset can be added from the plane by entering an offset value or by clicking and dragging it in the graphics window. The options for a simple section analysis are shown in Figure 5–9.

Figure 5–9

  - For an Advanced Section analysis, specify the number of sections and the section spacing (i.e., the distance between sections), as shown in Figure 5–10.

Figure 5–10

Step 3 - Define the options.

Once you have selected references for the analysis, you can define the options.

Zebra Analysis

For a Zebra analysis, select one of the three direction icons as shown in Figure 5–11. Select the direction that most clearly shows the transition between surfaces. You can leave it with the default direction first, define the other options, apply the analysis, and then edit the analysis to change the direction, as required. Adjust the Thickness, Density, Opacity, and Display Quality values to modify the proportion of white to black, number of stripes, transparency, and resolution for the zebra pattern, respectively.

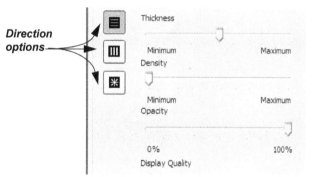

Figure 5–11

Draft Analysis

Enter minimum and maximum angles, as shown in Figure 5–12. Selected faces or quilts that fall between the specified angles will display in a color corresponding to the measured angle, based on the pull direction. Activate the **Gradient** option to display the color band as a continuous gradient, rather than discrete color bands. Adjust the display quality to control the quality of the color shown on the selected faces and quilts.

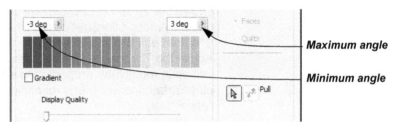

Figure 5–12

Curvature Analysis

To control the visual display of a curvature analysis you must manipulate the Comb Density, Comb Scale, and Surface

Density. The (Comb Density) option controls the spacing

between the spines. The (Comb Scale) option controls the

scale or length of the spines. The (Surface Density) controls the density of the sample curves for interior faces. In the Direction section, specify having the curvature comb display in Direction1, Direction2, or both. The options are shown in Figure 5–13.

Figure 5–13

Surface Analysis

Enter minimum and maximum curvature ratio values, as shown in Figure 5–14. Selected faces or quilts that fall between the specified curvature ratios display in a color corresponding to the measured curvature ratio. Click **Auto Range** to set the minimum curvature ratio to the smallest value found on the selected faces and the maximum curvature ratio to the largest value found on the selected faces. Activate the **Gradient** option to display the color band as a continuous gradient, rather than discrete color bands. Adjust the display quality to control the quality of the color shown on the selected faces and quilts.

Figure 5–14

Cross Section Analysis

With a Simple Section analysis, you can only change the section offset value and the direction. For Advanced, additional options enable you to specify minimum and maximum thicknesses, as shown in Figure 5–15.

Figure 5–15

Step 4 - Complete and review the analysis.

Click **Apply** to run the analysis. The analysis is added to the Model browser. Review the results to ensure that they display as required.

- Rotate the model, as required, to better view the results. Rotating the model for a Zebra analysis is particularly helpful in determining how well the stripe edges line up.

You might want to clarify or adjust the results by changing the direction(s) selected for a Zebra or Curvature analysis, or you might want to adjust the minimum and maximum values for a Draft, Gaussian, or Section analysis. Make adjustments, as required, and click **Apply**. Continue adjusting, as required, and click **Cancel**.

Step 5 - Display or edit an existing analysis.

To display an analysis you already created, double-click on it in the *Analysis* folder in the Model browser. The analysis result displays on the model. To toggle off the visibility of all analyses, right-click on the *Analysis* folder and select **Analysis Visibility**, as shown in Figure 5–16.

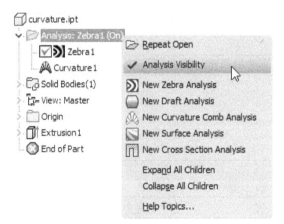

Figure 5–16

To edit an analysis you already created, right-click on it in the Model browser and select **Edit**.

Practice 5a

Analyzing Continuity

Practice Objectives

- Conduct a Zebra analysis that evaluates whether continuity exists between adjacent surfaces based on the results of stripes applied to the surfaces.
- Conduct a Curvature analysis that evaluates whether continuity exists between adjacent surfaces based on the results of flow lines that extend normal to the surfaces.

In this practice, you analyze a model using the Zebra and Curvature analysis tools. The Zebra analysis enables you to investigate the continuity between adjacent faces or quilts, while the Curvature analysis investigates the curvature of a face or quilt, as well as between boundaries.

Task 1 - Perform a Zebra analysis.

Perform a Zebra analysis to determine if continuity exists between surfaces.

1. Open **zebra.ipt**. Rotate the part to appear similar to that shown in Figure 5–17.

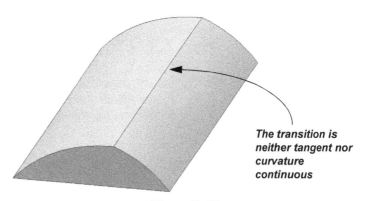

The transition is neither tangent nor curvature continuous

Figure 5–17

2. In the *Inspect* tab>Analysis panel, click ≫ (Zebra). The Zebra Analysis dialog box opens.

3. Keep the default name of **Zebra1**. In the Selection area, clear the **All** option. Select the two curved surfaces in the model.

---

4. Set the *Thickness* slider halfway between Minimum and Maximum, the *Density* slider at approximately 75%, the *Opacity* at 100%, and the *Display Quality* at 100%, as shown in Figure 5–18.

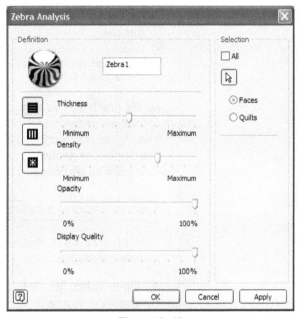

Figure 5–18

5. Click **Apply** to run the analysis while leaving the dialog box open. The model displays similar to that shown in Figure 5–19. Note how the stripes on any one face do not line up with the stripes on the adjacent face The orientation of the model affects the display of the results. Try and spin the model so that you obtain something similar to that shown.

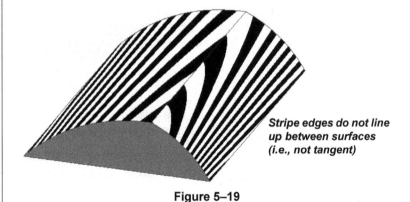

Stripe edges do not line up between surfaces (i.e., not tangent)

Figure 5–19

6. Close the Zebra Analysis dialog box. The analysis is listed in the Model browser, as shown in Figure 5–20.

Figure 5–20

7. In the Model browser, right-click on **Analysis:Zebra1 (On)** and select **Analysis Visibility**. This toggles off the display of the stripes on the model; however, the analysis remains in the model.

Task 2 - Change the tangency between the two curved surfaces.

1. Edit the sketch associated with **Extrusion1**.

2. In the *Sketch* tab>Constrain panel, click ⟨⟩. Select the two sketch entities shown on the left side of Figure 5–21 to make them tangent. Select the left edge first and the right second. The sketch updates as shown on the right side.

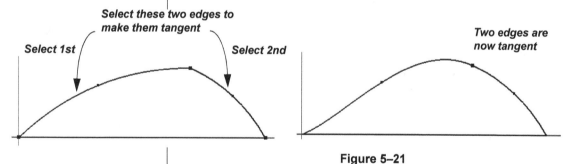

Figure 5–21

3. Finish the sketch.

4. In the Model browser, right-click on **Analysis:Zebra1 (Off)** and select **Analysis Visibility**. This toggles on the display of the stripes on the model, as shown in Figure 5–22. The stripes have updated to reflect the change in tangency between the two surfaces. They now line up with each other; however, they do not smoothly transition to the stripes on the adjacent face. There is an angle between the two.

Stripe edges line up between surfaces; however, there is a sharp angle (not continuous)

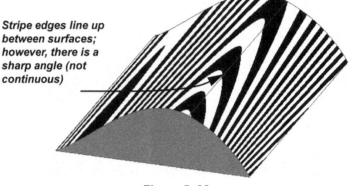

Figure 5–22

Task 3 - Change the continuity between the two curved surfaces.

1. Edit the sketch associated with **Extrusion1**.

2. In the *Sketch* tab>Constrain panel, click 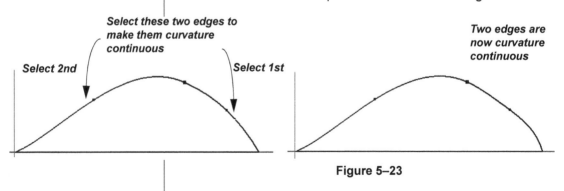. Select the two sketch entities shown on the left side of Figure 5–23 to make them G2 Continuous. Select the right edge first and the left second. The sketch updates as shown on the right side.

Select these two edges to make them curvature continuous

Select 2nd

Select 1st

Two edges are now curvature continuous

Figure 5–23

3. Finish the sketch. The stripes have updated to reflect the change in curvature continuity between the two surfaces, as shown in Figure 5–24. The stripes now line up with one another; and smoothly transition to the stripes on the adjacent face. There is no angle between the two.

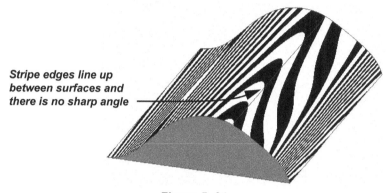

Stripe edges line up between surfaces and there is no sharp angle

Figure 5–24

4. Save the model and close the window.

Task 4 - Perform a Curvature analysis.

Perform a Curvature analysis to obtain a visual representation (in the form of a curvature comb) of the curvature on selected faces. In the next series of tasks, you will use the same model and similar steps to review non-continuous, tangent, and curvature continuity on surfaces.

1. Open **curvature.ipt**. The Zebra analysis has also been included in this model and is automatically toggled off when a model is initially opened.

2. In the *Inspect* tab>Analysis panel, click (Curvature). The Curvature Analysis dialog box opens.

3. Keep the analysis name as **Curvature1**. Select the two curved surfaces on the model, maintain the default settings, and click **OK**. The curvature spines are too small to easily see the curvature change between the two surfaces.

4. In the *Analysis* folder, right-click on **Curvature1** and select **Edit**.

5. Adjust the sliders for each option, as shown in Figure 5–25.

- (Comb Density): Controls the spacing between the spines.

- (Comb Scale): Controls the scale or length of the spines.

- (Surface Density): Controls the density of the sample curves for interior faces.

6. Click **OK**. The model displays as shown on the right side of Figure 5–25.

Move the sliders near these positions

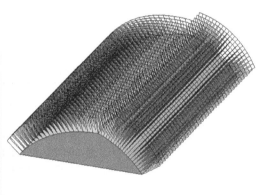

Figure 5–25

7. Orient the model to the Front view using the ViewCube. The model should display similar to that shown in Figure 5–26. Note that the curvature comb separates at the boundary between the two surfaces. This means that the two surfaces are discontinuous.

Separation of the curvature comb along the boundary indicates the adjacent faces are discontinuous (i.e., not tangent)

Figure 5–26

8. Using the sketching techniques previously discussed, apply tangency between the two surfaces. The Curvature analysis display updates, as shown in Figure 5–27. It might vary slightly based on the slider values that you set.

Continuation of the curvature comb with different lengths indicates that the adjacent faces are tangent (but not curvature continuous)

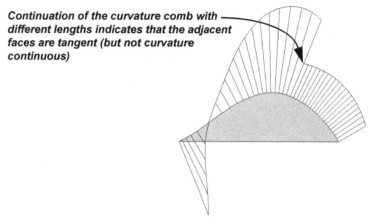

Figure 5–27

9. Using the sketching techniques previously discussed, apply curvature continuity between the two surfaces. Be sure to select the curves in the same order as was described earlier. The Curvature analysis display updates, as shown in Figure 5–28. It might vary slightly based on the slider values that you set.

Continuation of the curvature comb at the same length indicates that the adjacent faces are curvature continuous

Select 2nd.

Select 1st.

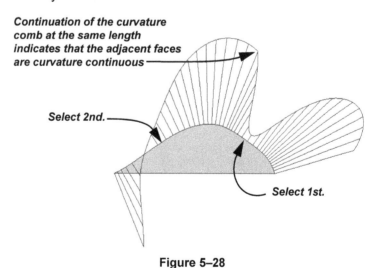

Figure 5–28

Task 5 - Activate and edit an existing analysis.

1. Currently, the **Curvature1** analysis is active. In the Model browser, double-click on the **Zebra1** analysis to activate it. The Zebra analysis displays on the model.

2. In the Model browser, right-click on **Zebra1** and select **Edit**. The Zebra Analysis dialog box opens with the current settings.

3. Increase the Density slider to the maximum value. Click **OK** to apply the changes and close the dialog box. The Zebra analysis updates with more stripes.

4. Right-click on the *Analysis* folder and select **Analysis Visibility** to toggle off the display of all analyses. The model displays without any visible analysis results.

5. Save the model and close the window.

Practice 5b

Draft Analysis

Learning Objective

- Conduct a Draft analysis that enables you to visually evaluate whether the applied draft values in a model are within a specified range.

In this practice, you analyze the draft on a model. The results of the Draft analysis are shown in Figure 5–29, where two distinct draft angles are detected.

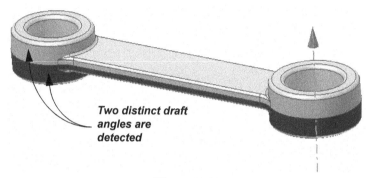

Two distinct draft angles are detected

Figure 5–29

Task 1 - Perform a Draft analysis.

1. Open **analyze_connecting_rod.ipt**. Orient the model as shown in Figure 5–30.

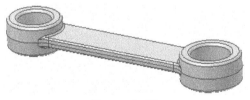

Figure 5–30

2. In the *Inspect* tab>Analysis panel, click (Draft). The Draft Analysis dialog box opens.

3. In the *Selection* area, clear the **All** option and verify that **Faces** is selected.

4. Select all 16 surfaces, including the opposite side's, as shown in Figure 5–31.

5. In the dialog box, in the *Pull* area, click 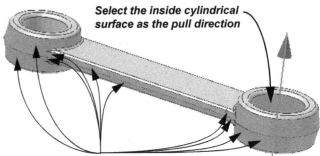 and select the inside cylindrical surface of one of the holes, as shown in Figure 5–31.

Select the inside cylindrical surface as the pull direction

Select all the side surfaces of the model to analyze, including the opposite side

Figure 5–31

6. Specify the start and end draft angles as **-1** and **1** degrees respectively, as shown in Figure 5–32.

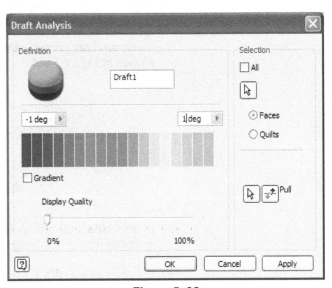

Figure 5–32

7. Click **Apply**.

8. The sides of the part turn two different colors, indicating that the draft angle is different on the top than the bottom. It might be difficult to identify from that shown in Figure 5–33. Compare the color on the model to that in the dialog box; you should be able to tell that the current draft angle on the model is outside of the +/-1 range.

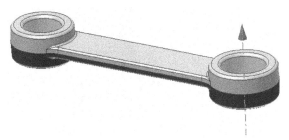

Figure 5–33

9. Click **Cancel**. In the next step you are required to change the range. You cannot reset the range without closing the analysis and editing it.

10. In the Model browser, expand the *Analysis* folder and double-click on **Draft1** to edit it.

11. Change the range to **+/-5** degrees and **Apply** the change. The colors on the model change and now indicate that the draft is within this range. If this is not accurate enough for you can continue to reduce the range or use other tools to measure or show the dimension on these surfaces.

12. Click **Cancel**.

13. Save the model and close the window.

Practice 5c | Section Analysis

Learning Objectives

- Conduct a Cross Section analysis that displays the model sectioned through a single plane.
- Conduct a Cross Section analysis that displays the model sectioned through a series of planes and also identifies areas of the model that conflict with specified maximum and minimum wall thickness values.

In this practice, you analyze the sections through a model using a simple section analysis and an advanced section analysis. The results of the analyses are shown in Figure 5–34.

Figure 5–34

Task 1 - Perform a simple cross-section analysis.

A simple cross-section analysis enables you to display the model sectioned through a plane on the part.

1. Open **section_analysis.ipt**. The model displays as shown in Figure 5–35.

Figure 5–35

2. In the *Inspect* tab>Analysis panel, click 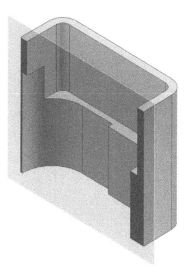 (Section). The Cross Section Analysis dialog box opens.

3. Keep the default name of **CrossSection1**.

4. On the left side of the dialog box, verify that (Simple) is selected. This enables you to conduct a simple cross-section analysis.

5. The XZ origin plane is already displayed. Select this plane.

6. Flip the direction of the cross-section. The arrow points in the direction where the material is to be removed.

7. Maintain the *Section Offset* value as **0 mm**.

8. Click **OK**. A cutaway view of the part based on the selected plane is displayed, as shown in Figure 5–36.

Figure 5–36

9. Clear the visibility of the XZ plane in the model.

10. In the Model browser, right-click on **Analysis:CrossSection1 (On)** and select **Analysis Visibility**. This toggles off the display of the active sectioned view of the model; however, the analysis remains in the model.

Task 2 - Perform an advanced cross-section analysis.

An advanced cross-section analysis is a more advanced analysis that enables you to define multiple section planes by either selecting or creating them, and verify their maximum and minimum wall thicknesses.

1. In the *Inspect* tab>Analysis panel, click (Section).

2. Keep the default name of **CrossSection2**.

3. On the left side of the dialog box, click (Advanced). This enables you to conduct an advanced cross-section analysis using the advanced options shown in Figure 5–37.

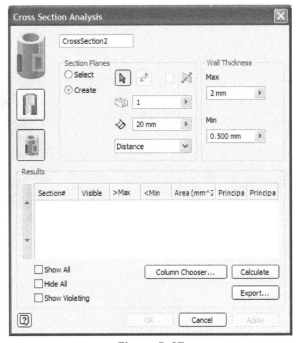

Figure 5–37

4. In this dialog box you can define whether to select an existing plane or create a new one. Keep **Create** selected and select the top plane, as shown in Figure 5–38.

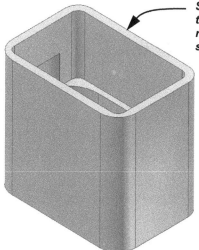

Select this top plane as the placement reference for the section plane

Figure 5–38

5. Click ⬆ to flip the direction of the section planes downwards into the model.

6. Change the measurement type from *Distance* to **Spacing**, enter **10** for the number of planes, and **10 mm** for the spacing between the planes. Set the *Max Wall Thickness* to **10 mm** and the *Min Wall Thickness* to **4mm**, as shown in Figure 5–39.

Figure 5–39

7. Click **Apply**. The model updates to display the cross-sections and the dialog box provides numerical data on the sections, as shown in Figure 5–40.

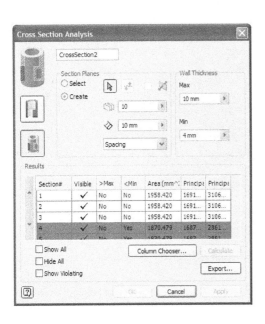
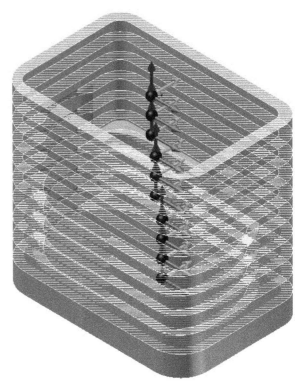

Figure 5–40

8. At the bottom of the dialog box, select **Show Violating**. This toggles off all sections that are within the min and max wall thickness restrictions. Note that seven sections remain. The blue highlighted areas on the model indicate where the wall thickness is smaller than required. The red highlighted areas indicate where the wall thickness is larger than required.

9. Review the list of sections at the bottom of the dialog box. The columns provide information on the section and whether or not it passes the wall thickness criteria that was specified.

10. Click **Cancel** to close the Cross Section Analysis dialog box. Leave the display of the Cross Section Analysis on so that as changes are made to the model, you can see the results in the analysis.

Task 3 - Edit geometry.

1. Edit **Sketch3** and change the 27.204 dimension to **24.5**.

2. Finish the sketch and note that the blue highlighted (min wall thickness) violations are gone.

3. In the Model browser, in the *Analysis* folder, double-click on **CrossSection2** to open the Cross Section Analysis dialog box. Only four sections remain that violate the wall thickness restriction.

Based on this design, there is no combination of dimensions for **Sketch3** that will satisfy both restrictions on the wall thickness. The design requires that the minimum thickness be met; however, the max thickness can be larger.

4. In the Cross Section Analysis dialog box, modify the *Max Wall Thickness* to **20 mm**. Click **Apply**.

5. At the bottom of the dialog box, select **Show Violating**. Now, there are no longer any sections in conflict.

6. Click **Cancel** to close the Cross Section Analysis dialog box.

7. Save the model and close the window.

Chapter Review Questions

1. Which of the following best describes the strips that are displayed when identifying tangent surfaces that are not curvature continuous in a Zebra analysis?

   a. Stripe edges that do not line up between surfaces indicate that the adjacent surfaces are tangent, but not curvature continuous.

   b. Stripe edges that line up between surfaces where there is a sharp angle are tangent, but not curvature continuous.

   c. Stripe edges that line up between surfaces where there is no sharp angle are tangent, but not curvature continuous.

2. Which of the following best describes the curvature comb that is displayed when identifying tangent surfaces that are also curvature continuous in a Curvature analysis?

   a. Separation of the curvature comb along the boundary indicates that adjacent faces are tangent and curvature continuous.

   b. Continuation of the curvature comb with different lengths indicates that adjacent faces are tangent and curvature continuous.

   c. Continuation of the curvature comb at the same length indicates that adjacent faces are tangent and curvature continuous.

3. Which Section analysis type enables you to analyze the min and max wall thickness for a single cross-section through the model?

   a. Simple Section Analysis

   b. Advanced Section Analysis

4. If the default comb spacing between splines is not sufficient to easily study curvature changes on a surface, which setting do you use to change it?

   a.

   b.

   c.

5. A Draft analysis was completed on a model using an acceptable range of +/- 3 degrees. If the color on one surface is outside the color gradient in the Draft Analysis dialog box, the draft on the model is within the acceptable range.

   a. True

   b. False

6. Match the Analysis Type in the left column to its icon in the right column.

Analysis Type	Icon	Answer
a. Zebra Analysis	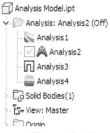	_____
b. Draft Analysis		_____
c. Surface Analysis		_____
d. Section Analysis		_____
e. Curvature Analysis		_____

7. Which of the following statements is true regarding the Model browser shown in Figure 5–41.

Analysis Model.ipt
  ∨ Analysis: Analysis2 (Off)
      Analysis1
      ☑ Analysis2
      Analysis3
      Analysis4
  Solid Bodies(1)
  View: Master
  Origin

Figure 5–41

   a. Analysis2 is the currently active analysis that is being displayed on the model.

   b. There are four analysis types that are currently being displayed on the model.

   c. Analysis4 is currently the active analysis, however, its visibility is not currently displayed on the model.

   d. There is no analysis being displayed on the model.

   e. None of the above.

Answers: 1.b, 2.c, 3.b, 4.a, 5.b, 6.(deabc), 7.d

Command Summary

Button	Command	Location
	Curvature Analysis	• **Ribbon:** *Inspect* tab>Analysis panel
	Draft Analysis	• **Ribbon:** *Inspect* tab>Analysis panel
	Section Analysis	• **Ribbon:** *Inspect* tab>Analysis panel
	Surface Analysis	• **Ribbon:** *Inspect* tab>Analysis panel
	Zebra Analysis	• **Ribbon:** *Inspect* tab>Analysis panel

Index